Cultural Diversity in Nursing:
Issues, Strategies, and Outcomes

Edited by
Jacqueline A. Dienemann,
PhD, RN, CNAA, FAAN

AMERICAN ACADEMY OF NURSING

Cultural Diversity in Nursing: *Issues, Strategies, and Outcomes*

The American Academy of Nursing was established in 1973 under the aegis of the American Nurses Association.

ISBN#: 1-55810-138-1
G-195

Published by:

AMERICAN ACADEMY OF NURSING
600 Maryland Avenue, S.W.
Suite 100 West
Washington, DC 20024-2571

Design and editorial services provided by C&W Creative Services.

Editorial services by Mollie Eulitt.

Contributors

Barbara J. Brown, EdD, RN, CNAA, FAAN, FNAP

Health Care Administration Consultant and Editor
Nursing Administration Quarterly
Aspen Publications
Germantown, Maryland

Helen M. Castillo, PhD, RN, CNA, FAAN

Professor and Chair
Department of Undergraduate and Graduate Nursing
College of Nursing and Health Sciences
The University of Texas at El Paso
El Paso, Texas

Noel J. Chrisman, PhD, MPH

Professor
Department of Psychosocial and Community Health Nursing
School of Nursing
University of Washington
Seattle, Washington

Catherine R. Davis, PhD, RN

Director of Research and Evaluation
Commission on Graduates of Foreign Nursing Schools
Philadelphia, Pennsylvania

Jacqueline A. Dienemann, PhD, RN, CNAA, FAAN

Associate Professor
Coordinator of Nursing Systems and Management
School of Nursing
The Johns Hopkins University
Baltimore, Maryland

Joyce Newman Giger, EdD, RN, CS, FAAN

Professor of Graduate Studies
School of Nursing
University of Alabama at Birmingham
Birmingham, Alabama

JoEllen Goertz Koerner, PhD, RN, FAAN

Vice President for Patient Services
Sioux Valley Health System
Sioux Falls, South Dakota

Beverly L. Malone, PhD, RN, FAAN

President
American Nurses Association
Washington, D.C.

Virginia M. Maroun, MSN, RN

Executive Director
Commission on Graduates of Foreign Nursing Schools
Philadelphia, Pennsylvania

Terry R. Misener, PhD, RN, FAAN

Professor
Department of Family and Community Nursing
College of Nursing
University of South Carolina
Columbia, South Carolina

Lillian H. Mood, MPH, RN, FAAN

Director of Risk Communication and Community Liaison on Environmental Quality Control
South Carolina Department of Health and Environmental Control
Columbia, South Carolina

Phyllis R. Schultz, PhD, RN, FAAN

Associate Professor
Department of Psychosocial and Community Health Nursing
School of Nursing
University of Washington
Seattle, Washington

Richard L. Sowell, PhD, RN, FAAN

Associate Professor and Chair
Department of Administrative and Clinical Nursing
College of Nursing
University of South Carolina
Columbia, South Carolina

Cheryl B. Stetler, PhD, RN, FAAN

Specialist for Nursing Research
Baystate Medical Center
Springfield, Massachusetts

Claudette G. Varricchio, DSN, RN, OCN, FAAN

Program Director and Nurse Consultant
Division of Cancer Prevention and Control
National Cancer Institute
Bethesda, Maryland

Contents

Preface

As health care's center of focus moves away from hospital-based care and toward primary care, clashes of culture inevitably will arise more frequently between health care providers and their patients and clients. Simultaneously, cultural clashes between workers also will increase in frequency due to the widening social distances between races, ethnicities, and socioeconomic classes in our society. These cultural clashes will be aggravated by stresses associated with the rapidity of change and the end of lifetime employment entitlements for workers in the United States. This dramatic change in the country's historic business environment creates a major barrier to the teamwork vital to maintaining business competitiveness.

This monograph will attempt to provoke its readers toward action in order to truly create new organizational cultures with innovative solutions to these teamwork barriers. In our view, an organizational climate that nurtures cultural competence is a necessity for survival in the business world of the future. By cultural competence we mean showing respect for the rights, preferences, cultural values, and mores of each individual coworker and client within the context of his or her reference group. We believe that cultural competence results in humane and effective behavioral interactions that are essential for organizational effectiveness and the achievement of desired outcomes.

This monograph is the third in a series being produced by the American Academy of Nursing's Expert Panel on Culturally Competent Care. The first monograph, Diversity, Marginalization, and Culturally Competent Health Care: Issues in Knowledge Development (Meleis et al. 1995), explored knowledge generation concerning the role culture plays in health and health care. The second monograph, Promoting Cultural Competence in and through Nursing Education (Lenburg et al. 1995), focused on education as a means to increase nurses' valuing of cultural diversity. This third monograph, Cultural Diversity in Nursing: Issues, Strategies, and Outcomes, deals with the interface of diverse cultures and the organizational structures in which we practice as clinicians, educators, researchers, and nontraditional nurses. Our goal is to highlight the critical nature of culture in the work of nursing. Cultural competence in nursing practice is compromised when care is delivered within the context of a monolithic dominant culture imposed upon all careers, corporate goals, and standards of care.

The cultural mix in the United States varies widely, but cultural diversity is universal. In 1987, the Hudson Institute released Workforce 2000: Work and Workers for the Twenty-first Century (Johnston and Packer 1987). This now famous study predicted that only 15 percent of the 25 million people expected to enter the U.S. work force between 1985 and 2000 would be white males, reflecting the changing demographics of the country. By 2020, the nation's ethnic minorities are expected to increase to 34 percent of the total population. In many parts of the country, African Americans, Asians, Native Americans, and/or Hispanics are, or soon will be, in the majority (U.S. News and World Report 1995). Going beyond ethnicity, cultural differences also may be related to age, disability, tenure of residence, sexual preference, or any other characteristic that sets a person or group apart from the dominant majority. Organizational cultures that only accept the worldview of the dominant western European majority offer ineffective atmospheres for providing health care to a variety of cultural groups (Airhihenbuwa 1995). Local solutions for attracting larger numbers of nonwhites to the health professions and for creating true partnerships between communities and health care providers are much needed in order to provide culturally appropriate care to all patients.

In order to guide our writings, the contributors to this monograph, as a group, agreed on certain basic assumptions about cultural diversity, including the following:

- Group identity may be based on phenotype, culture, or any other characteristic that a group shares which sets it apart from others. One person has many group identities.
- Prejudice, racism, stereotyping, and ethnocentrism are present in all work group situations.
- Heterogenous work groups may have higher intragroup conflict related to cultural diversity.
- The dominant subgroup is often ignorant of its own privilege.
- People tend to structure themselves into hierarchial groups, with power centered at the top. Collaboration and cooperation will not occur without incentives.

Our society values cultural diversity but not separatism. The valuation of various cultures within our society does not imply the devaluation of our nation as a whole. As Krauthammer (1995) warned, we must find a civil way out of the dilemma of being a nation of thoroughly intermixed cultures or go the way of the Balkans. Habayeb (1995) asserts that part of the dilemma is not recognizing that cultural diversity goes beyond color, religion, and geographic location, and that each person has a culture, a cultural heritage, and is culturally diverse.

One purpose of this monograph is to invoke reflection on cultural diversity within the reader's workplace. Some questions to aid reflection include:

- What multiple cultures do I represent?
- What personal actions on my part support a climate that values diversity?
- Within my workplace, how committed is

management to acknowledging the complexities of a multicultural work force and approaching them with a problem-solving attitude?

One way to encourage such reflection was to not speak with one voice in this monograph. We decided to use multiple authors with focused, but sometimes overlapping, chapters in order to emphasize the heterogeneous voices from differing cultures, localities, and workplaces. Some of the authors present research-based information and some present more personal observations based on experience. Each chapter concludes with a summary of issues presented, highlights of recommended strategies for action, and a "wish list" of preferred outcomes. A section entitled "Suggested Readings and Resources" is included at the end of the monograph to assist the reader in going beyond reflection to actually transforming the level of cultural competence in his or her own workplace.

Transformation, in our view, occurs through dialogue concerning the results of reflection and action on the culturally limiting situations encountered in the work environment (Freire 1973). This occurs best within a small group that offers critique, support, and encouragement. Thus, we also recommend that all readers form partnerships within their workplaces, with the goal of increasing their personal cultural competencies. This, in turn, will lead to reflection and action concerning how to change the work group, the entire organization, and the societal context in which it exists. The need for multilevel action will become evident as the reader explores why cultural incompetence exists within his or her own workplace and its negative consequences.

In the creation of this monograph, the authors discussed not only what to include but also how to present it. Since our intended audience is composed primarily of nurses in management, we assumed the reader has a basic knowledge of management theory and practice. We then agreed upon our vision of a culturally competent organization, which we defined as follows:

- A climate exists where persons of all ethnic, racial, and cultural identities may excel.
- Plural values are recognized, communicated, and influence decision making.
- Structure is integrated so there is no correlation of job status and group identity.
- Multiple groups participate in informal networks that offer support and job mobility.
- Institutional bias is eliminated.
- Cultural conflict is managed through training, management development, information, and communication (adapted from Cox 1994).

The organization of this monograph begins with a look at structural processes that impede or aid a climate which promotes cultural competence and culturally competent teamwork (Chapters 1 and 2). Next, the authors explore two specific types of cultures — gender and immigrants (Chapters 3, 4, and 5). These chapters go beyond the personal experiences of these minorities to the health policy implications. Then we turn to the personal cultural competence of American nurses who participate in intercultural consulting (Chapter 6). Returning to this country, we examine culturally competent practice and its implications for nurse administrators within today's rapidly changing environment (Chapters 7 and 8). Finally, we describe training for cultural sensitivity and analyze and describe examples of programs submitted by schools of nursing and health services agencies that are intended to increase cultural competence (Chapters 9 and 10).

We wish to thank the American Nurses Association and the American Organization of Nurse Executives for including calls for exemplars in their publications. We also thank the publications committee of the American Academy of Nursing for its support and significant critiques.

References

Airhihenbuwa, C.O. 1995. Health and culture. Thousand Oaks, Calif.: Sage.

Cox, T. 1994. Cultural diversity in organizations: Theory, research, and practice. San Francisco: Barrett-Koehler.

Freire, P. 1973. Pedagogy of the oppressed. New York: Continuum.

Habayeb, G. 1995. Cultural diversity: A nursing concept not yet reliably defined. Nursing Outlook 43 (5): 224-227.

Johnston, W.B. and Packer, A.E. 1987. Workforce 2000: Work and workers for the twenty- first century. Washington, D.C.: Hudson Institute.

Krauthammer, C. 1995. Quebec and the death of diversity. Time, November 13, p. 124.

Lenburg, C.B.; Lipson, J.G.; Demi, A.S.; Blaney, D.R.; Stern, P.N.; Schultz, P.R.; and Gage, L. 1995. Promoting cultural competence in and through nursing education: A critical review and comprehensive plan for action. Washington, D.C.: American Academy of Nursing.

Meleis, A.I.; Eisenberg, M.; Koerner, J.E.; Lacey, B.; and Stern, P. 1995. Diversity, marginalization, and culturally competent health care: Issues in knowledge development. Washington, D.C.: American Academy of Nursing.

U.S. News and World Report. 1995. Ahead: A mostly minority America. October 30, p. 23.

Cultural Diversity in Nursing:
Issues, Strategies, and Outcomes

Chapter 1
Improving Organizational Cultural Competence

Beverly L. Malone, PhD, RN, FAAN

Organizational diversity reflects differences in workers based on their membership in various groups (Carnevale and Stone 1994). Since individual differences can give rise to discord, such differences (whether within a corporate organization or one's family of origin) require adjustments, continuous reequilibrations of relationships and systems, and the ultimate sacrifice of setting aside one's own perspectives to acknowledge and value the perspectives of another. Acknowledging and valuing difference is a difficult and often painful task. Perhaps the most painful step for the dominant group within an organization is admitting when others have been wronged. This is equally true for the nursing profession and nursing organizations that speak of inclusion and opportunity, while reality shows poor representation of cultural diversity among providers, managers, and leaders (Malone 1993a).

To offset the potential chaos caused by diversity, differences must be embraced by organizations in order to achieve a sense of community and shared design of living (Carnevale and Stone 1994). Embedded in the acknowledging and valuing of differences is the assurance that every member of the community has access to all available economic and career opportunities. Wong (1991, p. 48) states that "diversity without community is anarchy."

This chapter will provide a brief review of the structural barriers to valuing diversity within organizations, and will offer strategies for change. As a strategy to promote organizational diversity, affirmative action

is discussed as a case example, although it has proven to be an ineffective model for transforming organizational culture from a monolithic framework dominated by white males to one of diversity. However, affirmative action efforts are important steps that can serve as a transitional bridge to valuing and managing diversity. Other relatively new strategies will be described as pivotal to the transformation of organizational cultures. Finally, issues related to the valuing and managing of cultural diversity by nursing and nursing organizations will be explored.

Affirmative Action: A Strategy of Diversity

If diversity is a source of chaos, why would an organization choose to diversify? Cox (1994) suggests that there is a moral imperative — it is the right thing to do. However, this moral imperative alone has not been exceedingly successful in changing organizational cultures. The Equal Employment Opportunity (EEO) and affirmative action initiatives of the 1970s provided legislative and regulatory motivation for organizational diversity within the corporate world. Diversity became a federal issue related to civil rights, with rewards and punitive contingencies. Thomas (1990) lists five premises on which affirmative action was established:

1. White, adult males make up the business mainstream in the United States.

2. The U.S. economic edifice is a solid, internationally dominant institution with more than enough space for everyone.

3. Women, African Americans, immigrants, and other minorities should be allowed into the business main stream as a matter of public policy and common decency — a moral imperative.

4. Widespread racial, ethnic, and sexual prejudice keeps minorities out.

5. Legal and social coercion are necessary to bring about change.

Affirmative action and EEO efforts, however, were not effective enough for the organizations targeted, nor for the minorities and others identified as intended beneficiaries. The dominant culture continued to view "difference" as frequently meaning less capable and less desirable.

Assessing Old Strategies for New Times

Since the 1970s, the United States has discovered that its economic edifice is not as solid or unchanging as previously believed, and U.S. corporations are scrambling to compete more successfully in foreign and domestic markets. Women, ethnic minorities, and immigrants have entered into corporate life at increasing rates over the past 20-30 years and have dramatically changed the diversity of the U.S. work force. Although entry remains a critical problem, the new issue of access to every level of the organizational structure is equally significant. Demographics indicate growing percentages of nonwhites in the U.S. population, with white males becoming a minority of those entering the work force; however, white males still dominate the top echelons of corporations (Johnston and Packer 1987). In addition, the force of the moral imperative has been superseded by a narrow focus on profitability and the continued existence of corporations. Economic realities demand new inclusive strategies that fully engage the human resource potential of every member of the organizational work force. This logically leads to an economic imperative for valuing and managing cultural diversity.

Thomas (1990) suggests that the necessity of business survival has succeeded in overcoming racial, ethnic, and gender prejudices to unlatch the doors of organizational entry that once were barred by these attitudinal perspectives. While legal and social coercion play an important role in facilitating opportunities for diversity to grow, they have never assured integration into the fabric of the organization for those who are perceived as different, nor provided protection from informal backlash to unwanted entry. Affirmative action, for example, is now perceived as injurious by every individual who feels unfairly passed over, and acts as a stigma for those identified as beneficiaries (Thomas 1991).

While affirmative action has played a significant role in moving ethnic minorities, women, and immigrants into mainstream corporate America, the need for new strategies to overcome perceived injustices and assure career opportunities is evident. It is less clear what new strategies should be adopted. The next step, however, must involve creating a corporate culture that provides entry and upward mobility for all kinds of people. Experts on cultural competence within organizations suggest moving toward strategies of valuing and managing diversity (Thomas 1991; Cox 1994; Carnevale and Stone 1994; Senge 1990).

According to Carnevale and Stone (1994, p. 24), "Valuing diversity means being responsive to a wide range of people unlike oneself." Such responsiveness requires the recognition that other people's standards, perspectives, and values are as valid as one's own. The concept of a "wide range of people" includes, but is not limited to, race, ethnicity, gender, class, native language, national origin, physical disability, age, sexual orientation, religion, professional experience, personal preferences, and individual work styles.

Managing diversity demands a continual process of planning, implementation, and evaluation of strategies to achieve the desired goals of diversity. Managing diversity subdues the chaos that can evolve without appropriate direction and the support of a potentially volatile mix of differences.

When organizations manage diversity, the valuing of diversity is implemented throughout the entire system, with initiatives at all levels of the organization.

Cox (1994) describes managing diversity as orchestrating an organization to maximize the potential benefits of diversity and minimize the potential disadvantages. Carnevale and Stone (1994) suggest that through valuing and managing diversity, organizational cultures can be transformed. The next section presents an overview of strategies to implement the managing and valuing of diversity in organizations.

Strategies to Manage Diversity

Strategies to manage diversity emphasize the need for changing the organizational environment, rather than trying to change people, in order to develop a transformed organizational culture of diversity (Cox 1994; Thomas 1990; Jamieson and O'Mara 1991; Loden and Rosener 1991; Malone 1993a; Fernandez 1991).

Jamieson and O'Mara (1991) suggest the development and implementation of "flex-management." This strategy utilizes four central approaches: (1) matching people and jobs, (2) managing and rewarding performance, (3) informing and involving people, and (4) supporting lifestyle and life needs. In order to implement these approaches, systems, policies, and procedures must be changed to incorporate organizational values and a corporate mind-set that values diversity.

In addition to changing the structures and management practices of organizations, training activities are needed to assist individuals working within the organization to value their own and others' cultures, and to gain skills in managing diversity for productivity enhancement. This is accomplished through programs in awareness training and skill-based training (Carnevale

and Stone 1994). Battaglia (1992) identifies four critical skills for creating a collaborative work environment among diverse employees:

1. cross-cultural understanding,

2. intercultural communication, including verbal and nonverbal deciphering and communication,

3. conflict management, and

4. a flexible willingness to try new behaviors and embrace change.

Awareness training is aimed at heightening awareness of diversity issues and exploring an employee's unexamined assumptions and tendencies to stereotype. This cognitive exercise focuses on facts and reflection. For instance, Thiederman (1991) recommends having managers study the cultures relevant to their employee composition and adjust their management practices accordingly. Malone (1993b) warns against limiting training to cognitive awareness. One potential danger lies in making people more aware of differences and problems without providing any skills or solutions to the dilemma. This increases nonproductive conflict. Another danger is that people may assume specific facts are general truths about all members of a cultural group — e.g., all women are primary caretakers of their children and therefore cannot assume demanding business positions. A third danger arises if training programs are designed for specific cultural groups and are not updated when new arrivals change the cultural mix.

Skill-based training should follow awareness training. Such training engages the learner in an active assessment of skill-building ability, reinforces the use of existing skills, and offers learning opportunities in diversity interaction skills (Carnevale and Stone 1994). Overall, cultural transformation may be achieved by utilizing a model based on an adaptation of Thomas's (1990) work, which includes seven foci of action for management to undertake:

1. Clarify Your Motivation — The most useful motivational discovery is that learning to manage diversity will make the organization more competitive (Eubanks 1990), reflecting the diverse marketplace and work force that already exists. Reliance on social and moral imperatives, even with legal incentives, is insufficient and creates a limited commitment to change.

2. Audit Your Corporate Culture — Define your corporate reality. Collect statistics on employee characteristics, functional areas, years in service, years between promotions, etc. Assess the budget for resource allocations for valuing and managing diversity. Create matrices that illustrate the corporate mix (e.g., gender, race, first degree, birthplace, etc.). Collect phrases that embody corporate images and beliefs (e.g., "the cream will rise to the top"; "we are a family"; "we cannot lower our standards"; etc.). Have a task force with multicultural representation review how these phrases reflect or fail to reflect the valuing of cultural diversity. Through this process, unstated assumptions underlying the corporate culture can be identified.

3. Clarify the Organizational Vision of Corporate Culture — The most productive vision of diversity employs a full engagement of the human resource potential of the total work force. This needs to be operationally implemented in order to demonstrate a clear commitment to change (Morrison 1992; Lowenstein and Glanville 1995). Alternative visions that have not demonstrated success in transformation include: (1) the clustering of ethnic minorities and women on a low plateau of the organization, with only a few who

are fully admitted to the upper strata; and (2) an emphasis on heightened sensitivity, with executives "generously allowing" ethnic minorities and women to work at all levels of the organization. This vision results in second-class status for ethnic minorities and women, resulting in high turnover rates and the attachment of a stigma of beneficence to those who remain.

4. Expand Your Goal — The goal of transformation is not the creation of a melting pot, where each person is assimilated into the dominant culture. Rather, the objective is to create a new heterogenous culture that recognizes each person's worldview. The concept of culture is seen as more than race or gender, and is critical to understanding the potential contribution of each employee. Develop a strategic plan, based on a philosophy of inclusion of differences and with a sense of purpose, that transcends the interests, desires, and preferences of any one group. Have the plan reviewed for cultural domination by differing members of identified groups within your organization. Set definite, numerical, meaningful goals and review progress regularly to maintain momentum (Morrison 1992).

5. Modify Your Assumptions — Corporate culture contains the same basic assumptions that drive any organization. It is important to realize that these assumptions are unexamined and have not been consciously chosen. One step toward cultural transformation is the corporate audit, in which assumptions driving the current culture are examined. A second step is to determine what must change in order for diversity to be valued and associated conflict to be positively managed (Thomas 1991).

6. Continue Affirmative Action — Expanding beyond affirmative action does not negate the continuing need to include it in your strategic plan. In order to operationalize a corporate culture that values diversity, diversity must first exist throughout the organization. This usually requires recruitment, retention, development, and promotion strategies that are responsive to emerging issues.

7. Implement Training — Senge (1990) describes a learning organization as one that constantly expands its capacity to create its future. He differentiates adaptive learning for survival and generative learning for growth. Awareness-based and skill-based training, implemented within the strategic plan for total system change, are necessary elements for transformation.

The Nursing Profession and Nursing Organizations

In this section, the application of the expanded model presented above is applied to transforming nursing's organizational culture. It begins by examining whether nursing's moral imperative to value and respect patients extends to valuing and respecting all members of the profession. It then outlines what nursing as a profession must do in order to fulfill its moral imperative for all nurses.

Clarify Nursing's Motivation

As the altruistic guardian of a vital social service, nursing has always been professionally identified and guided by a moral imperative. In its philosophy, nursing asserts the mandate to care for all people, regardless of race, color, creed, or religion. In order to be operationalized, this philosophy of valuing and respecting diversity also must extend to others within the profession of nursing (Malone 1993a). However, as stated earlier, there is a disparity between nursing rhetoric and nursing reality. For example, 89 percent of the 2.1 million employed nurses are white; this figure has not substantially changed over the past 10 years (Moses 1996).

Nursing appears to have hidden behind its shield of a moral imperative for patient care and denied the current reality of the lack of diversity within its ranks and organizational structures, from institutions of educational instruction to those of health care delivery. In clarifying nursing's motivation, however, nursing leadership must accept that the American corporate dilemma is also a nursing dilemma. With this acceptance comes the acknowledgment that organizational diversity of nursing services should be a reality and a goal. In service to local and global communities, nursing must learn to value and manage diversity for the survival and growth of the profession.

Audit Nursing's Organizational Culture

To conduct an assessment of the current value placed on diversity by the nursing organization within an institution, Malone (1993a) suggests auditing the philosophy, negative assumptions, budget, and accountability of the nursing organization. Begin by comparing the written vision statements and philosophies of both the institution and its nursing organization. Language in both should address the nursing organization's commitment to cultural diversity. The importance of the institution's goal to achieve a culturally diverse work force should be reflected in the nursing organization's guiding principles.

The second step is to examine the corporate culture for negative, unexamined assumptions that are part of the unwritten philosophical foundation shaping organizational behavior. For example, in reviewing the qualifications of ethnic minority and male applicants, is an assumption that "achieving goals of diversity means lowering standards" revealed?

Since the budget is an annualized model for allocating resources to meet goals identified in the strategic plan, the budgetary existence of funded activities and resources to facilitate inclusion of diverse people in the work force and transform the organizational culture is a good indication of the degree of commitment to change. The budget implements the nursing organization's vision statement, philosophy, mission statement, and strategic plan. Determine if monies for inclusion programs, minority recruitment efforts, cultural competence workshops, or other activities to implement stated goals are included.

Finally, the audit must ask the question, "How does this organization assure accountability for demonstrating a commitment to a culturally diverse work force and valuing and managing diversity?" Start with a review of the strategic plan for process and outcome evaluation criteria. Are the goals measurable? Is there a responsibility chart, including names? Does the timetable include dates for progress reports? A second source of information is the annual report — is diversity progress reported in it?

Another source of information on commitment to cultural competence is the nursing organization's written policies. Do policies state a commitment to managing diversity? What internal opportunities exist for minority employees to gain educational and experiential credentials for promotion? Do policies and procedures reflect adaptation to patients' and/or students' cultural differences? How do rewards and sanctions reflect a commitment to valuing diversity? For instance, are valuing and managing diversity included as evaluation criteria for salary increases? Looking at performance evaluation tools to determine whether activities associated with cultural diversity are a line item on each individual's evaluation form also can be revealing.

Clarify Nursing's Vision

The clarification of nursing's vision is intricately tied to the values held by nursing leadership. Nursing leaders must examine their own ideas of organizational cultural diversity. Is the image one of minorities being assimilated into the dominant culture? Such an image is a limited view that is more an adaptive, short-term strategy than a generative one that will transform the organizational culture (Senge 1990). Nursing's vision must be one that values and manages diversity, providing an opportunity to fully tap the potential of all members of the nursing organization.

The nursing organization's vision for valuing and managing diversity should be evident in the strategic plan. Patient care goals should include the utilization of cultural factors critical to promoting healing and health. Professional goals should address attracting and valuing nursing personnel from a variety of cultures. All goals should be clearly delineated, with projected times, dates, and numbers and identification of the primary individuals responsible for implementation and evaluation.

Expand Nursing's Goal

Nurses need to recognize the relationship between the health of diverse groups and their representation within the health professions. For instance, the disparity in health status between African Americans and whites in American society is well-known (Fingerhut and Makuc 1992). However, while 12.5 percent of the country's overall population is African American, only 4.2 percent of nurses are African American clinicians, leaders, and policymakers (U.S. Public Health Services 1992). A template for organizational transformation that includes the valuing and managing of diversity would provide a magnet for attracting representative numbers of African Americans, as well as other minority groups. This, in turn, could contribute to the development of culturally appropriate interventions to improve the health status of diverse populations within our country.

Nursing's focus also must stretch to include global differences, as well as relationships with different disciplines. Changes in global communication and the mobility of both professionals and patients increasingly requires cultural competence. Additionally, health care is rapidly becoming more complex, requiring increased interaction between different disciplines. Nurses also are increasingly responsible for overseeing the work of technicians with differing educational levels, adding more diversity to the work group delivering care. No longer can the profession restrict its focus to just nurses and nursing, but must articulate nursing's uniqueness, demonstrate a capability for building a sense of community, and transform systems to utilize the potential of every member — regardless of group identity or culture — in order to deliver competent patient care.

Modify Nursing's Assumptions

The modification of negative underlying assumptions is necessary for the transformation of nursing's organizational culture. For instance, recognizing that an assumption that diversity involves a lowering of standards might be interwoven with the recruitment, retention, and graduation of nurses in our schools of nursing would be the first step toward changing this assumption.

The exposure of this assumption and its historical roots, revealing the homogeneous models used in arriving at this belief, may assist the nursing organization in revising its assumptions. Nursing organizations must begin to realize that, by valuing and managing diversity, the same or higher productivity levels can be achieved with a heterogeneous student body or work force. Learning to value individual competence within a cultural context, to acknowledge the unique perspectives that differing cultures offer, and to develop the ability to build a sense of community are critical skills for the nursing profession.

Another commonly held assumption — one that often is not recognized as negative — is that competent professional nurses are color-blind. The pride that nurses espouse in being color-blind prevents any acknowledgment or valuing of differences, effectively eliminating the possibility of becoming more culturally aware and competent.

Continue Affirmative Action

Since 1980, nursing has not improved in its statistical representation of cultural diversity within the profession (Villeneuve 1994). The need for actions that provide entry and career mobility for minority nurses remains a high priority. Nursing cannot discontinue affirmative action until it actually is more diverse. Meanwhile, care delivery involves an increasingly diverse professional and paraprofessional work force, presenting a challenge for nurse administrators to transform their organizations in order to value and manage diversity. Unfortunately, there is little evidence that health care organizations are successfully making this transition. A recent study of six health care institutions found that the institutions could not be characterized as proactively managing diversity. Instead, they were assessed as pluralistic organizations with compliance-oriented strategies that only addressed routine human resource management practices (Muller and Haase

1994). Health care organizations, in relation to valuing and managing diversity, are drastically lagging behind organizations in many other industries.

Implement Training

Awareness-based and skill-based training, described earlier, are powerful learning models that can facilitate a nursing organization's successful transformation into a learning organization. These learning models positively relate to team building, total quality management, and empowerment (Carnevale and Stone 1994).

Conclusion

The critical steps for transforming nursing's organizational culture from monolithic white female organizations to heterogeneous ones are:

1. assessing and acknowledging the current reality,

2. creating a vision of the desired future, and

3. based on the disparity between current and desired states, developing organizational processes to bridge the gap.

The logic of these steps is simple, but their effective implementation requires the nursing profession to change its assumptions and behavior related to cultural diversity. This requires a major commitment, with continued persistence and support. The ultimate goal is to develop an environment that is conducive to the ability of all work force members to contribute their greatest potential through the recognition, valuing, and management of diversity. In the process of reaching this goal, nursing has the opportunity to embrace the chaos of differences and transform health care delivery and educational systems into communities of diversity.

Summary of Issues

1. American health care institutions lag behind many other institutions in their incorporation of the valuing and managing of diversity.

2. Current nursing policies and behaviors do not reflect adequate valuing or managing of diversity.

3. Although affirmative action has not been fully effective, it is a useful tool for increasing minority access to employment.

4. Nursing continues to be primarily a white, female-based occupation.

Recommended Strategies

1. Include initiatives in strategic plans for transforming organizational behavior in order to value and manage diversity.

2. Assist dominant cultural groups within health care organizations and schools of nursing to acknowledge their privileged position and to recognize the harm of forcing the assimilation of minority groups.

3. Identify the underlying negative assumptions within nursing that are barriers to valuing and managing diversity.

4. Implement skill-based training in order to grow beyond mere awareness of difference to the active valuing and managing of diversity.

5. Continue legislation that supports affirmative action programs.

6. Establish benefits, such as tuition reimbursement, that allow employees to advance their educational qualifications for entering and/or advancing within the health professions.

Preferred Outcomes

1. Health care organizations will implement training in order to transform corporate culture so that it values and manages cultural diversity.

2. Nursing will reward practice that is culturally appropriate, collaborative, and values difference.

3. Nursing will seek members who are culturally diverse and culturally competent.

4. Nursing will reflect the demographics of the country in its membership.

References

Battaglia, B. 1992. Skills for managing multicultural teams. Cultural Diversity at Work 4 (3): 4.

Carnevale, A. and Stone, S. 1994. Diversity beyond the golden rule. Training and Development Journal 31 (10): 22-39.

Cox, T. 1994. Cultural diversity in organizations: Theory, research, and practice. San Francisco: Barrett-Koehler.

Eubanks, P. 1990. Workforce diversity in health care: Managing the melting pot. Hospitals (June): 48-51.

Fernandez, J. 1991. Managing a diverse work force. New York: Lexington Books.

Fingerhut, L.A. and Makuc, D.M. 1992. News from NCHS. American Journal of Public Health 82: 1168-1170.

Jamieson, D. and O'Mara, J. 1991. Managing workforce 2000: Gaining the diversity advantage. San Francisco: Jossey-Bass.

Johnston, W.B. and Packer, A.E. 1987. Workforce 2000: Work and workers for the twenty-first century. Washington, D.C.: Hudson Institute.

Loden, M. and Rosener, J. 1991. Workforce America! Managing employee diversity as a vital resource. Homewood, Ill.: Business One Irwin.

Lowenstein, A.J. and Glanville, C. 1995. Cultural diversity and conflict in the health care workplace. Nursing Economic$ 13 (4): 203-209, 247.

Malone, B. 1993a. Caring for culturally diverse racial groups: An administrative matter. Nursing Administration Quarterly 17 (2): 21-29.

. 1993b. Shouldering the responsibility for culturally sensitive and competent health care. Imprint (Sept./Oct.): 53-54.

Morrison, A. 1992. The new leaders: Guidelines on leadership diversity in America. San Francisco: Jossey-Bass.

Moses, E. 1996. Unpublished data from the March 1996 National Sample Survey of Registered Nurses. Division of Nursing, Bureau of Health Professions, Health Research and Services Administration, Department of Health and Human Services, Rockville, Md.

Muller, H.J. and Haase, B.E. 1994. Managing diversity in health services organizations. Hospital and Health Services Administration 39 (4): 415-433.

Senge, P. 1990. The fifth discipline. New York: Doubleday.

Thiederman, S. 1991. Profiting in America's multicultural marketplace. New York: Lexington Books.

Thomas Jr., R. 1990. From affirmative action to affirming diversity. Harvard Business Review 68 (2): 107-117.

. 1991. Beyond race and gender. New York: American Management Association.

U.S. Public Health Service. 1992. U.S. census data, 1990. Washington, D.C.: U.S. Government Printing Office.

Villeneuve, M.J. 1994. Recruiting and retaining men in nursing: A review of the literature. Journal of Professional Nursing 10 (4): 217-228.

Wong, F. 1991. Diversity and community. Change 23 (July/Aug.): 48-52.

Chapter 2
Culturally Competent Teamwork

Joyce Newman Giger, EdD, RN, CS, FAAN

Lillian H. Mood, MPH, RN, FAAN

As our nation's health care system is being restructured to create teams of professional and technical workers to provide care, the topic of culturally competent teamwork becomes more salient. The likelihood of various ethnic groups being represented within these teams increases as the heterogeneity of the U.S. population grows. Such teams are likely to be diverse in occupation, power, social status, life experience, ethnicity, and cultural makeup. The ability of these teams to work productively together is dependent, therefore, on the cultural competency of each member.

Very little is found in the literature on working with staff from diverse cultures or on building effectiveness among culturally diverse teams. Designating tasks and functions within a culturally competent team involves not only an understanding of competencies and delegation, but also of c ultural fit. There is even less written on the relationship of culturally competent teamwork to the delivery of care to clients from other cultures (Giger and Davidhizar 1995; Spector 1996; Andrews and Boyle 1995). In order for health professionals to provide culturally appropriate care, it is essential to understand specific factors that may influence individual patient behavior. This same concept must be applied to building effective teams when working with staff from culturally diverse backgrounds.

Fostering the acceptance and valuing of difference among members of a culturally diverse health care team may prove to be an arduous task. However, the changing makeup of team members in the work force will necessitate an understanding of cultural diversity if work force issues are to be adequately addressed. In fact, by 2000, 92 percent of the growth in this country's work force will be the result of an increase in the number of women, ethnic minorities, and recent immigrants. In addition, 70 percent of the work force will be composed of minority groups (e.g., African Americans, Hispanics, Asians, etc.). If the projections on employment trends hold constant, 34 percent of all employed workers in the United States will speak English as a second language by 2000 (U.S. Department of Commerce 1996). Therefore, it is essential for health care teams to learn to understand, accept, and value the cultural differences within their memberships.

It is important to remember that each member of the health care team must be viewed as an essential component of the team. The health technician's work is as important to team functioning as is that of the physician. Health care professionals not only must work arduously to delegate tasks to team members prepared to carry out the tasks, but also must work at building cohesion among team members representing the rapidly changing heterogenous climate of the United States.

Culture and Diversity

To develop an appreciation for the uniqueness of members of a culturally competent team, it is necessary to understand the cultural values, beliefs, and practices of particular groups. This information often is not included in professional health care education, or it is provided in isolated lectures that students do not view as relevant to "real" health care education on specific tasks.

In its broadest sense, culture can be defined as the values, beliefs, norms, and practices of a particular group that are learned and shared, and which guide thinking, decisions, and actions in a patterned way (Leininger 1985). Values often are sustained by culture and, consequently, govern the actions and decisions of those within a cultural group. If culturally competent teamwork is to be actualized, it is essential to utilize cultural assessment as the necessary first step toward building cohesion.

Culture can and often does give meaning to behaviors that might otherwise be judged negatively (Giger and Davidhizar 1995). For example, the nurse with a Chinese heritage standing "too close" to the nurse with a European heritage may not intend to appear threatening, but they both may be reacting to differences in a personal definition of appropriate private space. Misunderstandings may lead to accusations by the latter nurse that are bewildering to the former nurse, and cause discord between them. Health care team members need to realize that cultural beliefs, values, and worldviews not only may be different between themselves and their clients, but also among themselves. Taking action to clarify why people act as they do will contribute to the resolution of problems when they arise. Each health care provider must act responsibly and must learn to value and appreciate the cultural uniqueness that each individual brings to the health care environment.

Diversity often accentuates the quality of the work performed by a culturally competent health care team. Often, team members who are of an ethnic minority are expected to act as experts on the culture and health practices of their group of origin. This may be an unfair burden if the team members are acculturated and not knowledgeable about specific ethnic health practices. Alternatively, a person often can draw from his or her knowledge based on lived and learned experiences concerning culture and cultural beliefs. Sharing this knowledge with other members of the health care team

can help to build cultural competence. The problem occurs when team members do not incorporate new knowledge or gain independence in caring appropriately for clients from ethnic minorities. It is best to combine both the lived and learned experiences of each member to enhance the performance of the team.

Cultural Assessment

To build a culturally competent health care team with team cohesion, it may be necessary to hold retreats in order to build cultural understanding among members of the team. One element of such retreats should be learning to use practical cultural assessment tools. Recently, transcultural nursing theories have begun to appear in the literature; however, few practical, adequate assessment tools and methods to accompany application have been developed. Giger and Davidhizar (1991, 1995) present a systematic approach that can be helpful in building culturally competent teams. This model encompasses six cultural phenomena, which include:

1. communication,

2. space,

3. social organization,

4. time,

5. environmental control, and

6. biological variation.

These six cultural phenomena will be used in this chapter as a framework for discussing strategies to build harmony and encourage culturally competent teamwork.

Communication

Communication can and often does create the most insurmountable barrier among health care team members. This is particularly evident when working with clients and staff from diverse backgrounds. Communication can be perceived as the combination of all thought and human interaction. Communication also provides the very mechanism by which individuals connect. Thus, communication and culture are intrinsically and indelibly linked. Because communication is critical to building culturally competent teams, it is essential that health care managers and clinicians learn the art of effective communication techniques. This includes awareness of racial, ethnic, cultural, and social factors that influence communication.

One method for increasing communication awareness is for team members to visit places where a different ethnic community gathers — on the community's own turf — watching and listening as they communicate and conduct business with each other. Another method is for team members to observe the interactions among ethnic groups other than their own, while visiting the company cafeteria, for example. The critical elements of communication to observe are dialect; style; volume and silence; use of touch; context of speech, including emotional tone; and kinesics, including gestures, stance, and eye behavior. Each of these elements will vary among and across cultural groups, but cultural patterns may be identified (Poole, Giger, and Davidhizar 1995).

A lack of understanding of these cultural patterns may lead to misinterpretations of the meaning of behavior. For example, Asian Americans tend to speak softly, while African Americans, German Americans, and Irish Americans have a tendency to amplify speech volume (Giger and Davidhizar 1991). A coworker might interpret softness of speech as evidence of timidity, indecisiveness, lack of assertiveness, or incompetence, when none are true. This lack of verification of the meaning of behavior may reduce team functioning, as well as restrict the career advancement of those whose culture has standards of behavior that differ from the dominant culture.

Although people may speak the same language, establishing communication remains difficult. In English, words have both a denotative and a connotative meaning. Denotative refers to the meaning derived from typical usage by most people who share the language; connotative refers to the meaning derived from an individual's personal experience. The connotative meanings of words for both the sender and receiver may vary based on life experiences and learning. It is important, therefore, when offended by another's use of a particular word or confused by the use of a word seemingly out of context, to identify if cultural differences are contributing to a misunderstanding. Giger and Davidhizar (1995, pp. 34-38) offer guidelines to help develop effective communication within a multicultural health care team:

1. Assess the personal beliefs of members.

2. Assess communication variables from a cultural perspective.

3. Modify communication patterns to enhance communication.

4. Identify mannerisms that may be threatening and avoid using them.

5. Understand that respect for others and the needs they communicate is central to positive working relationships.

6. Use validating techniques when communicating.

7. Be considerate of a reluctance to talk when the subject might involve culturally taboo topics, such as sexual matters.

8. Use team members from a different culture as resources, but do not support a dependency by the team on those members.

9. Support team efforts to plan and adapt care based on the communicated needs and cultural backgrounds of individual patients.

10. Identify potential interpreters for patients whenever necessary in order to improve communication.

Silence is yet another important cultural consideration in communication. Silence may be thoughtful or it may indicate that an individual has nothing to say. In conversation, silence may relate to stubbornness, resistance, apprehension, discomfort, or none of these. Silence on the part of Russian, French, or Spanish individuals may signify agreement, but for some other cultures, silence may indicate disagreement. For some cultural groups, silence is undesirable and its presence may make others uncomfortable, resulting in attempts to fill every moment with conversation. However, within groups such as Native Americans, Chinese Americans, and Japanese Americans, silence is valued as respectful and viewed as essential to demonstrating an understanding of individual needs (Giger and Davidhizar 1995). It is important to clarify the meaning of silence when it occurs in culturally mixed groups, and to not act on stereotypical assumptions and generalizations that may not apply to specific situations.

Space

Space refers to the physical distance required in personal relationships, and the intimacy techniques utilized when relating verbally and nonverbally to others. Hall (1966) identified four distinct zones of appropriate interpersonal space that various cultures define differently:

1. intimate,
2. personal,
3. social consultative, and
4. public.

Generally speaking, persons in the dominant white American middle class prefer a personal distance between people of two to three feet. For other cultural groups, such as African Americans and the French, this space may be considered distant and generally unacceptable. These differences in personal space needs may cause discomfort, and telling others of this discomfort will promote mutual understanding and adjustment. Keeping appropriate distance in relationships is critical to developing group cohesion (Spector 1996).

Social Organization

For some cultural groups, the family unit is the single most important social organization. For these groups, family matters may take on more significance than personal, work, or national issues. This view differs from the dominant paradigm in the United States, which defines personal, work, or national needs as paramount. Therefore, culturally competent work policies should provide flexible guidelines on leave in order to respect this difference in social organization.

Holistic family values may be found among Chinese, Mexicans, Vietnamese, and Puerto Ricans, who define family as more than the nuclear unit; in fact, it includes persons beyond bloodlines, creating large, extended families. Thus, using a day off to travel to visit a grandmother's ill sister may surprise others on the team who have a different cultural orientation. Further, having an entire extended family take off work and take children out of school to attend a minor in-house award ceremony for a team member also may surprise coworkers. Yet, the meaning of the award for that person might only be achieved by the support and presence of the entire extended family. Cultural differences in such matters need to be identified in order to be understood (Andrews and Boyle 1995).

Among some cultural groups, such as Appalachian people, reliance on family for advice and assistance is of utmost importance. A staff member from such a culture may need to leave suddenly to advise or assist a family member. This differs from the dominant culture, in which the emphasis is placed on individual self-reliance (Giger and Davidhizar 1995).

Part of multicultural teamwork involves realizing that others' values and priorities for the use of time are legitimate and need to be acknowledged in planning schedules, defining use of personal days, and covering the provision of patient care. Harmony will be promoted by not disparaging others' choices for self, family, or work, and by allowing flexibility for such choices.

Time

For most individuals, regardless of cultural heritage, the concept of time is familiar and is usually represented by a clock or calendar. However, it is important to remember that not everyone values clock time the same. Many cultural groups are actually scornful of clock time as a way to arrange social appointments, meals, etc. (Spector 1996).

Another dimension of time is an orientation to the past, present, or future. For people who are past-oriented, there is a tendency to value tradition and stability. For those who are present-oriented, meeting current demands is the top priority. The dominant cultural group's orientation is primarily future-oriented: all past and present activities are valued mainly for their contribution to the achievement of future goals, which is the single standard for success. Future-oriented staff are also task-oriented and disparage the use of time for exploring alternatives, accommodating another's pace, and displaying social support (Giger and Davidhizar 1995). Such staff members tend to view those who "waste time" in these

ways as passive and disorganized. Helping such individuals to become aware of the strengths of avoiding early closure on decisions and the time savings of inclusive strategies to implement change may assist them in learning to value difference. Assigning tasks to fit with personal time orientation can enhance productivity.

Environmental Control

Environmental control refers to the perceived ability of an individual within a cultural group to plan activities to control nature or direct environmental factors, thereby promoting feelings of security. Individuals who value this control are referred to as having an internal locus of control. They are often the impetus for strategic planning and implementation of planned change. In contrast, others believe that controlling nature is not possible or desirable, and that changes occur by fate, luck, or chance. These team members have an external locus of control. When forced to participate in control activities such as managing change, those with an external locus of control focus on intervening against obstacles, rather than active promotion of change. They often attribute success to serendipitous opportunity and creativity. Staff members who hold this orientation also may view planning for career advancement as unfruitful. Such individuals may believe that job promotion is directly related to factors outside their control and that activities such as annual goal setting are a waste of time (Giger and Davidhizar 1995).

Attachment to place is a concept associated with environmental control. Many cultures are linked with adapting and living in a certain terrain, climate, and location. For many people, their sense of well-being, wholeness, and health is associated with living in a certain place, especially when several generations of family also have done so. This can affect a team member's willingness to travel, commute long distances, or relocate (Andrews and Boyle 1995).

Biological Variation

Some genetic biological differences have been identified among gender, racial, and ethnic groups, and among groups sharing geographic heritages (Andrews and Boyle 1995). Differences in typical body structure, such as height and build, usually do not have a deleterious relationship to job performance. Managers should discourage unsubstantiated stereotypical judgments — e.g., women are rendered overly emotional by hormones, or Asian Americans are genetically predisposed to being mathematical experts. However, health care team members should recognize genetic biological variation as a risk factor for susceptibility to certain diseases among patients from specific ethnic, gender, or cultural groups. The delivery of culturally competent care includes being aware of these differences, assessing for them, and adapting interventions to minimize risk from disability and disease. For instance, being aware that mongolian spots are common in nonwhite infants and are not related to bruises commonly associated with child abuse is an example of culturally competent awareness. Incorporating such training in grand rounds and continuing education will facilitate cultural competence in professional practice.

Conclusion

This chapter summarizes the cultural factors that influence the behavior of each person in his or her daily life. The variations in behavior resulting from these factors need to be recognized, respected, and incorporated into company policies and work practices in order to facilitate effective teamwork among individuals with differing backgrounds. Employee training, staff meetings,

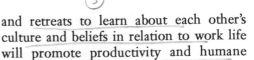

and retreats to learn about each other's culture and beliefs in relation to work life will promote productivity and humane working conditions.

Summary of Issues

1. With system restructuring, health care is increasingly being delivered by teams composed of multiple professions, power levels, ethnicities, and cultures.

2. The ability of members of multicultural health care teams to work productively together is dependent on the cultural competence of all members.

3. Cultural competence usually is not an integral part of the curriculum preparing for entrance into the health professions and technical positions.

4. Positive working relationships will not occur without specific actions by both managers and staff members to become aware of, respectful of, and responsive to cultural differences.

Recommended Strategies

1. Use staff retreats to guide cultural assessments of self and other team members.

2. Use staff meetings and grand rounds to inform the team of different cultural patterns and health and illness practices associated with various cultures.

3. Develop policies and procedures that reflect an awareness that behavior is culturally determined and that include the dimensions of communication, space, social organization, time, environmental control, and biological variation. Any or all of these may be the basis for differences among team members.

4. Avoid team dependency on ethnic minority members as assumed experts on their own or other cultural groups.

5. Foster the valuing of diversity through an ongoing assessment and validation of the cultural appropriateness of team interactions and acknowledgement of differences.

6. Include consideration of competencies and cultural fit in the delegation of tasks and functions to team members.

Preferred Outcomes

1. Health care teams will utilize all members' lived and learned experiences in planning and delivering health care.

2. Health care teams will foster mutual trust and respect of difference among members.

3. The contribution of each team member to the productivity of the team will be acknowledged and valued.

4. Members of all cultures will become more aware of the cultural basis for others' differences, and not judge them as inferior.

5. Team members will communicate discomfort when others violate their cultural norms, and will explore options that will be mutually acceptable for future interactions.

6. A learning climate will be maintained where members observe others' cultural patterns of behavior, as well as ask for cultural interpretations of differences.

References

Andrews, M.M. and Boyle, J.S. 1995. Transcultural concepts in nursing care, 2nd ed. Philadelphia: J.B. Lippincott.

Giger, J. and Davidhizar, R. 1991. Transcultural nursing: Assessment and intervention. St. Louis: Mosby Year Book.

. 1995. Transcultural nursing: Assessment and intervention, 2nd ed. St. Louis: Mosby Year Book.

Hall, E. 1966. Hidden dimension. New York: Doubleday.

Leininger, M. 1985. Transcultural care diversity and universality: A theory of nursing. Nursing and Health Care 6 (4): 209-212.

Poole, V.; Giger, J.; and Davidhizar, R. 1995. Delegating to transcultural teams. Nursing Management 26 (8): 33-34.

Spector, R. 1996. Cultural diversity in health and illness, 4th ed. Norwalk, Conn.: Appleton & Lange.

U.S. Department of Commerce, Bureau of Labor Statistics. 1996. Quarterly labor reports: October 1, 1995 to December 31, 1995. Washington, D.C.: U.S. Government Printing Office.

Chapter 3
Gender and Sexual Orientation Issues Among Nursing Personnel

Richard L. Sowell, PhD, RN, FAAN
Terry R. Misener, PhD, RN, FAAN

Addressing issues of cultural diversity is particularly challenging in the delivery of health care. Efforts to achieve cultural competence must focus equally on members of the health care team, health care providers, and consumers. The situation is further complicated by having no single accepted definition of what constitutes cultural diversity or who is included in efforts to achieve culturally competent health care. In addressing issues of cultural diversity, authors have focused on the presence or inclusion of individuals of differing racial and ethnic groups, religious beliefs, nationalities, and/or geographic heritages (Bowler 1993; Malone 1997; Habayeb 1995; Fitzpatrick and Whall 1989; Sorofman 1986). Focusing on such groups and their unique characteristics represents a necessary first step in striving for culturally competent health care. However, approaching cultural competencies by focusing only on such groups and their characteristics neither accurately acknowledges the diversity found in the work setting nor provides an understanding of the interactions observed in these settings.

Traditional approaches to cultural diversity and to the development of a culturally aware work force have, in the authors' observations, consistently ignored the importance of gender role and sexual orientation as sources of diversity and potential conflict in the work environment. Although nursing prides itself on taking a leadership role in addressing cultural diversity, there is limited nursing focus on gender and sexual orientation differences in the context of cultural diversity. This is not to discount the number of nursing authors who have examined variations in career mobility, comparable worth compensation, and professional autonomy in health care based on gender and sex role assignment. Consideration of gender and sexual orientation issues, however, has not been specifically addressed within a cultural framework nor linked to efforts to achieve culturally competent health care. It is important for nurses to fully recognize gender differences, sexual orientation, and sexual preferences as characteristics that interact with and cut across other cultural groupings that are based on race, ethnicity, nationality, or geographic heritage.

Therefore, our discussion in this chapter will seek to promote awareness of gender and sexual orientation issues within the health care work force, and to explore the impact of such issues on the work environment of nursing personnel. Further, we will argue the need to address gender role and sexual orientation in any meaningful approach to issues of culturally competent health care.

Gender Issues in Nursing

Historically, many of the first providers of nursing care were men who belonged to religious orders (Christman 1988a). Since the advent of modern nursing in the mid-19th century, however, women have dominated the delivery of nursing services. Today, of the 2.2 million registered nurses in the United States, only about four percent (88,600) are men (Squires 1995). The fact that nursing remains predominantly a female profession has personal and career ramifications for both females and males in nursing (Christman 1988a; Egeland and Brown 1988).

Nurses work within a health care hierarchy that remains patriarchal and empowers physicians and health care administrators to control the boundaries and context of nursing practice (Brown 1983; Hall 1993). Cummings (1995) asserts that the evolution of nursing as a female profession within a physician-dominated health care system reflects the socialization of women in a male-oriented society. Variations in sexual role and gender socialization between men and women form the foundation for what might appropriately be viewed as cultural differences between men and women based on role assignments, behavioral expectations, and what is deemed appropriate work for each group in society. Williams (1993) observes that jobs are clearly divided into men's work and women's work. Such classifications are most frequently based on stereotypes concerning beliefs about gender traits rather than actual biological differences between men and women (Cummings 1995; Powell 1993).

One of the clearest examples of such gendering of work can be seen in the role and status differences between physicians and nurses in the health care system (Williams 1993). Further, within the health care status hierarchy, there are rigidly reinforced mechanisms that discourage interoccupational mobility despite gender (Kissick 1966). Women or men who cross over into an opposite gender-dominated occupation challenge accepted gender assumptions embedded in the work and risk sanctions (Williams 1993). In nursing, not only do women frequently face scrutiny when moving into management or leadership positions, but men who enter the profession often encounter suspicions and questions about their masculinity or their intentions toward female patients. This represents a paradoxical reality that continues to support a gender-related segregation of occupations within health care.

Gender differences between men and women exist, and the way that each group approaches nursing differs. These gender differences must be recognized and appreciated, rather than ignored or devalued.

Women in Nursing

Undeniably, women have been and continue to be faced with gender role stereotyping in the workplace. Even with increasing numbers of women entering previously male-dominated fields such as law, medicine, engineering, and the clergy, most women continue to work in female-dominated occupations (Powell 1993). This may be due, at least partially, to the fact that jobs in our society are developed with gender expectations or cultural assumptions related to gender built into the work (Williams 1993). A number of authors have noted that the value placed on various occupations closely reflects the balance of gender traits (masculine versus feminine) deemed necessary to perform the work (Cummings 1995; Powell 1993; Williams 1993).

If gender traits and gender role expectations substantially influence the composition and status of occupations, it becomes important to examine feminine gender traits to determine their impact on work done by women. Stivers (1991) identifies caring, passiveness, intuitiveness, nurturing, and relationship orientation as traits associated with women. These traits are in sharp contrast to the traits of decisiveness, independence, and aggressiveness frequently equated with effective leaders. Such a view of women and leadership would imply that women will not be successful in positions where tough-mindedness and bold actions are needed. Herein, however, lies the problem of stereotyping individuals or groups. First, both women and men bring a variety of characteristics and talents to their work. The way these attributes are operationalized in the context of the requirements of the work will determine the degree of success achieved. The degree to which all leadership requires attention to relationships and nurturing of constituents underscores the values of these proposed "feminine" traits. Conversely, there is no basis for believing that individual women do not possess the ability to undertake decisive actions based on objective data analysis. The critical care nurse who is required to frequently make split-second, life-or-death decisions does not reflect the passive stereotype of women. However, the ability to take decisive action when needed does not preclude that same nurse from exhibiting caring and compassion for patients and their families. To portray gender characteristics in dichotomous gender stereotypes does not reflect reality and is particularly limited in its usefulness in the delivery of health care. Bem (1974, 1977, 1981) labels the ability of both men and women to use a full repertoire of behavioral attributes as androgyny. The most effective nurses, then, would seem to be those who are androgynous rather than those possessing the narrower range of attributes for only women or men. Caring and the ability to create a healing environment transcend gender and form the underpinnings of all health care occupations.

Women who aspire to leadership positions in health care organizations, however, face potential challenges both in achieving such positions and in maintaining their self-identification once in these positions. Despite advances made as a result of Equal Employment Opportunity initiatives that quadrupled the number of women, African Americans, and Hispanics in management positions between 1970 and 1989, many women continue to encounter elusive barriers in achieving top management positions. These seemingly intangible barriers form what has been termed a "glass ceiling" (Morrison and von Glinow 1990). The power and politics of health care remain in the hands of a relatively small group, consisting mostly of men. Social gender role assumptions and gender stereotypes have been skillfully used to maintain women in service or low-level management positions where they have little power or mobility (Brown 1983; Butter et al. 1987; Dipboye 1987; Morrison and von Glinow 1990).

Even for those women who do break through the glass ceiling, there seems to exist a complex task of demonstrating competency without abandoning the very traits that identify them as women (Stivers 1991; Edwards and Lenz 1990). In examining 232 female and 117 male chief nurse executives, Borman (1993) found that female executives reported higher levels of role strain and conflict between their personal and work lives than did male executives. The fact that women who achieve success in positions of organizational leadership are often accused of becoming more "male" than "female" provides a conflicting message about success and a negative reward for achieving success. In nursing, gender-negative rewards are not always generated by men or from outside the profession. For example, I recently inquired why a colleague had not been chosen by her peers to fill a leadership position in a nursing organization. The response I got was that there was concern that this individual was too easygoing and relationship-oriented. The group was concerned that such attributes would not serve the business of the organization well. While this most likely represents a less than complete explanation of the situation, it served to give rise to the question: Do nurses themselves view supposed feminine gender characteristics as being inconsistent with leadership and effectiveness?

Stivers (1991) suggests that there are two distinct approaches to women and leadership in feminist writings. The first approach is to adopt, at least pragmatically, the masculine characteristics thought to define leadership in society. The goal is to demonstrate that leadership characteristics such as decisiveness, boldness, and independence are not inherently male. The second approach focuses on showing that the unique qualities of women are consistent with achieving organizational objectives and that the culture of organizations needs to change, not women. From the latter perspective, it would seem that nurses, as the largest group of health care providers, may be in an excellent position to influence such a change in the culture of health care organizations. However, before such an initiative can be successful, more nurses will need to fully embrace the value of a woman's way of knowing and leading.

Men in Nursing

Although the percentage of men in nursing rose from 3.3 percent to 4.8 percent between 1988 and 1996, nursing remains a gender-segregated profession (Moses 1996). After a quarter century of feminism, equal work opportunity legislation, and multicultural initiatives, nursing in the United States continues to be dominated by middle-class white women (Bullough 1997). Further, this female domination of nursing has remained relatively constant during a period when a number of qualified men have been displaced from more traditional male jobs and are seeking new work opportunities. Why, then, have more men not viewed the nursing profession as a viable career option?

If gender stereotyping has served to keep women in traditionally female jobs, such as nursing, it has served to keep men out. The traits of "caring" and "nurturing," frequently identified as essential components of the nursing role, are sometimes cited as unique feminine qualities. This stance can make men in nursing or those considering nursing uncomfortable (Bullough 1997). Can a

man be an effective nurse, exhibiting such supportive characteristics, and still be a "real man"? While the answer to this question would seem obvious in an enlightened society, role strain among men in nursing is a reality (Egeland and Brown 1988). Men who enter the nursing profession frequently encounter the assumptions that they are either homosexual or not smart enough to become physicians. Such prejudices persist despite the lack of evidence to support such views. Yet, the fact that many men in nursing choose technically oriented specialties such as critical care and anesthesia may represent an effort to reconcile a desire to enter nursing with socialized gender role expectations (Gordon, Herrick, and Benvenutti 1994; Perkins, Bennett, and Dorman 1993).

A second factor that impedes the recruitment and, to a lesser degree, retention of men in nursing is discrimination (Kerswell and Booth 1995; Keeter 1994). Porter-O'Grady (1995) describes the reverse discrimination encountered by men in nursing as hitting the "concrete ceiling." This characterization is clearly meant to draw a contrast between the career plights of men and women, and to the "glass ceiling" often encountered by women in career fields in which they are a minority. Discrimination against men within nursing may have its roots in the very advent of the profession in the modern era. Kalisch and Kalisch (1986) propose that the vision of nursing held by Nightingale had no place for men. Such a view may not frequently be overtly expressed, but it may linger covertly in nursing education and practice. The sheer number of articles in the nursing literature that focus on the presence of men in management positions, question the appropriateness of male nurses in areas such as obstetrics, and scrutinize the differences between male and female students suggests a hypersensitivity to men in the profession

(Buchan 1995; Bullough 1993; Krausz et al. 1992; McKenna 1991; Okrainec 1994; Ryan and Porter 1993; Sherrod 1991; Snavely and Fairhurst 1984; Streubert 1994; Williams 1995). Porter-O'Grady (1995) suggests that the discrimination encountered by men in nursing is based on the existing power and political relationships within the health care system. That is, the dependency on, inequity in, and internal competition for relatively low-status positions within nursing are sources of discrimination that affect both male and female nurses. Such discrimination may be more readily recognized by men and perceived as inherently unacceptable based on their male gender role socialization or experiences within a male-oriented society.

However, to deny the existence of reverse discrimination or to view sexism in the nursing profession as merely an unavoidable result of overall discrimination against women is naive and does not foster realistic strategies to address the issue in the work environment. There is a need to acknowledge the existence of potential gender bias against men in nursing. The awareness of gender as a cultural component that demands attention in the management of work groups can be a first step toward fostering work equality and opportunity for all nurses. As Christman (1988b, p. 75) states:

> No one race, gender, or ethnic group has a monopoly on the qualities of intelligence, scientific competence, imagination, empathy, tenderness, concern for others, or motor skill ability. To state otherwise is to deny reality.

Nursing will benefit tremendously when each of its members internalizes the profession's articulated sensitivity to cultural diversity and acts as a role model for nondiscrimination in education, practice, and administration.

Sexual Orientation

Sexual orientations that differ from the prevailing norm are not new. Throughout history, homosexuals have been ridiculed, harassed, and treated differently from those citizens who were perceived as "normal." Attitudes regarding sexual orientation are surrounded by a cloak of silence on one hand, and outright discrimination on the other hand (Young 1988). Any treatise on cultural diversity in the workplace would be remiss if the issue of sexual orientation were not addressed. In this section, we will discuss the professional implications of sexual orientation (i.e., being gay or lesbian) in the workplace, specifically within the nursing profession.

During the past 30 years, much progress has been made in the area of equal opportunity and human rights in the workplace. Discrimination due to a person's race, ethnic background, religion, and/or disability is acknowledged as unacceptable; discriminatory behavior is grounds not only for negative personnel actions but also for legal confrontations. The issue of civil rights based on sexual orientation, however, has not reached parity with other antidiscriminatory practices (Greenhouse 1986; Sartorelli 1994). Zeidenstein (1990) summarized the sanctions faced by lesbians, for example, as including employment discrimination, court custody battles, housing discrimination, rejection by family and friends, violation of due process, physical violence, and antigay rhetoric.

In a country that espouses equal opportunity for all and a separation of church and state, these very precepts are often ignored where sexual orientation is concerned. Gays and lesbians are commonly denied opportunities afforded to almost every other segment of society. Furthermore, conservative Christian dogma often is used to condemn those whose sexual orientation is counter to strict interpretations of the Bible, despite a constitutional right to separation of church and state.

The knowledge of most health care workers concerning sexual orientation and cultural aspects of sexuality varies from ignorance to very limited. The social and health implications of sexuality often are absent from their professional education. The HIV/AIDS epidemic and its prevalence among gay men has recently forced the issues of sexual orientation and sexuality to be addressed, but often only within the context of the disease. Nursing textbooks and curricula continue to contain little or no content regarding sexual orientation and sexuality (Martindale and Barnett 1992).

Nursing prides itself on the fact that caring is a central theme in the conceptual paradigm of the profession. Yet the literature abounds with reports of ignorance, insensitivity, and outright discrimination against clients and fellow workers who are gay or lesbian. Negative behaviors toward homosexuals by caregivers have been documented to include poor care (Flint et al. 1986), avoidance (Meisenhelder 1994; Reed, Wise, and Mann 1984), and even violence (Lankewish 1987).

The attitudes of health care providers toward both homosexual colleagues and patients are abundantly documented in the literature (Garnets and D'Augelli 1994; Schwanberg 1990). In a comprehensive literature review of attitudes toward homosexuality in health care, 61 percent of the 59 articles reviewed on the subject showed negative attitudes toward gays and lesbians. More importantly, the study showed a shift from neutral to negative attitudes had occurred, and warned of the implications for patient care (Schwanberg 1990). Smith (1992) similarly finds that stereotyping of homosexual behaviors may negatively affect the care of the homosexual patient, stating that nurses must be comfortable with their own attitudes toward sexuality in order to provide quality care for patients with sexual orientations different from their own.

Frequently, gays and lesbians have been treated with insensitivity, antagonism, and discrimination in their health care encounters (Stevens and Hall 1991; Taylor and Robertson 1994). Peate (1995) admonishes nurses to be aware of the stigma placed on homosexual patients and to take care that their own values and belief systems are not imposed on clients, in order to avoid potentially harmful outcomes. Several studies further document that fear, ignorance, and homophobia influence nurses' ambivalent feelings and decisions to refuse care, particularly to patients with HIV/AIDS, both in the United States and other countries (Eakes and Lewis 1991; Huerta and Oddi 1992; Krasnik et al. 1990; McCann 1995; Scherer, Wu, and Haughey 1991; Young, Henderson, and Marx 1990).

Several studies in the literature indicate that nurses fear dealing with homosexual clients (Kim and Perfect 1988; Steinbrook et al. 1985; Young 1988). Douglas, Kalman, and Kalman (1985) studied homophobia among physicians and nurses. Of the 114 respondents, six identified themselves as either bisexual or homosexual. All indicated that they had personally cared for a male homosexual with AIDS. The majority of all respondents reported working with a homosexual colleague and/or having a close friend or relative who was homosexual. While both groups had a low-grade homophobic score on the Index of Homophobia scale (developed by the authors), the results revealed that nurses were significantly more homophobic than physicians. An equal number of physicians and nurses (32 percent) agreed with the statement, "In the hospital, patients with AIDS receive inferior care compared to patients with other illnesses." Physicians (32 percent) and nurses (30 percent) agreed with the statement that they "feel more negatively about homosexuality since the emergence of the AIDS crisis." Admitting the limitations of the study, the investigators remained confident about several conclusions: (1) men in the study had lower homophobic scores than women; (2) having a close friend or relative who was gay produced significantly lower homophobic scores; and (3) in contrast to nurses, physicians' personal anxiety was not reduced if they worked closely with a gay colleague.

In another study of 160 registered nurses in one London hospital, Lewis and Bor (1994) report that 54 percent of the nurses felt embarrassed when discussing sexuality with patients, although more than 78 percent of the nurses felt adequately educated regarding sexual matters. Male nurses were more likely to discuss sexuality with patients than were female nurses. The authors conclude that although knowledge is increased through educational programs, a strong negative affective component may still exist. They posit that educational programs for nurses should deal more effectively with bias and judgmental approaches to sexuality. This study reports on areas of concern and problems similar to those found by earlier writers, who documented the belief that an overemphasis had been placed on cognitive elements, along with a neglect of the affective and behavioral elements surrounding homosexuality (Martindale and Barnett 1992; Plasek and Allard 1984).

How prevalent is homosexuality among health care workers, and nurses in particular? Most estimates are deemed to be low because of an unwillingness by gays and lesbians to disclose their sexual orientation. However, recent work reported by the Department of Health Policy and Management of the Harvard School of Public Health (Sell, Wells, and Wypij 1995) can be used to extrapolate the figures. Sell and associates used the Project HOPE International Survey of AIDS-Risk Behaviors to make estimates for the United States, the United Kingdom, and France. These investigators used identification with both the definitions "homosex-ual sexual contact" and "sexual attraction to a member of the same sex" to derive their figures. They report that within the five years before the 1990 data collection, 6.2, 4.5, and 10.7 percent of males and 3.6, 2.1, and 3.3 percent of females in the United States, the United Kingdom, and France, respectively, reported having sexual contact with a member of the same sex. When the investigators expanded their definition of homosexual orientation to include sexual attraction toward a member of the same sex since age 15, in addition to sexual contact with a member of the same sex, the percentages rose to 20.8, 16.3, and 18.5 percent for males and 17.8, 18.6, and 18.5 percent for females in the United States, the United Kingdom, and France, respectively.

We assume that nurses are a cross section of the culture and representative of the national statistics. The registered nurse population in the United States is estimated to be between 1.8 and 2.2 million, with four percent of those being men (Squires 1995). Therefore, using two million as the number of registered nurses in the United States, and applying Sell and associates' percentages to the nursing population, we would expect to find that more than 77,500 have had sexual contact with a member of the same sex within the past five years [females=72,000; males=5,500], and 374,000 nurses [females=356,000; males=18,400] could be estimated as having a sexual attraction to a member of the same sex at some time since the age of 15. Stated another way, one out of every six nurses is estimated to have had a same-sex attraction since the age of 15. Although the majority of gay and lesbian nurses may not disclose their sexual orientation, these extrapolations, if correct, represent an impressive minority in the profession, and therefore demand attention in developing workplace antidiscrimination policies.

In 1978, the American Nurses Association passed a resolution to support civil rights legislation at the local, state, and federal levels; support that would ensure equal protection to all persons, regardless of sexual orientation and affectional preferences (American Nurses Association 1978). However, gays and lesbians often remain quiet about their sexuality to avoid discriminatory practices that would preclude them from being hired or advancing in the nursing profession. Fears of reprisal include personal safety and professional sanctions (Deevey 1993). Nurses' fears do not begin with their entry into the profession, but are reflections of their past experiences and awareness of happenings in society today.

The continuance of "gay bashing" demonstrates the reality of these fears (Freiberg 1987). In a study of 125 lesbians and gay men in a university community, D'Augelli (1989) found that 26 percent had been threatened with violence and 17 percent reported damage of personal property, with roommates most often implicated as those responsible. A study of U.S. teenagers (Remafedi 1987) found that 30 percent had been the recipient of physical abuse, 55 percent reported verbal abuse from peers, and 37 percent admitted being discriminated against because of their sexual orientation.

Why are gay and lesbian nurses unwilling to reveal their sexual orientation with their colleagues? Nurses are not deaf. Why should they believe that they would be treated any differently or thought of any more highly than the patients about whom their colleagues talk? They have heard the uncaring comments made by fellow workers concerning gay and lesbian patients, although jokes about sexuality, race, and religion are grounds for negative personnel actions (Rose 1993). It can seem at times that few people in the workplace are sensitive to the rights and feelings of colleagues who are gay and lesbian.

According to one study (Rose 1993), those who have "come out" state that it is easier when their colleagues have known and respected them as professionals before learning of their sexual orientation. Although one nurse in the study who disclosed her lesbianism felt it strained her relations with a fellow student: "I sense she fears being labeled as a dyke" (p. 51). In the same report, the majority of respondents reported hearing lesbianism "referred to as an illness or as deviant, and described as sinful by other nurses," and others recount "being passed over for promotion" because they are lesbians (p. 51). In another example, a lesbian nurse reported being denied compassionate leave when her long-term girlfriend became ill and died. Likewise, the stress placed on lesbian respondents was evident by almost three-quarters admitting they consistently censor themselves when discussing social activities with colleagues. This has implications both personally and professionally for lesbian nurses. Attitudes toward lesbian colleagues can easily be transferred to lesbian clients. Rose concludes that everyone in the study had encountered disrespectful behavior toward herself or other lesbians, and that a wide gap exists between the policy espoused by nurses and the attitudes and behaviors they encounter in the workplace.

The data reveal that homosexual nurses are discriminated against in the workplace. The stress caused by this discrimination surely must affect the ability of these nurses to interact with colleagues and render the highest levels of care. Yet, given the population estimates that approximately one out of every six registered nurses in the United States has likely had sexual contact with a member of the same sex during the past five years or has had a sexual attraction to a member of the same sex since puberty, sexual orientation is not a subject that can be denied, but one that must be dealt with in the workplace. Ignoring this issue neither facilitates its resolution nor fosters cultural competence among nurse administrators.

Conclusion

Habayeb (1995) acknowledges that attempts to address cultural diversity in the work environment require an awareness of the holistic influence of the complex interaction of culturally based characteristics, values, and behaviors. Cultural sensitivity must be based on the understanding that each member is a source of diversity and brings differing characteristics to any work group. When individuals sometimes spend more waking hours in the workplace than in their own homes, the workplace should provide a safe environment for diversity, including diversity related to gender and sexual orientation. Nonbiased attitudes regarding sexual orientation should be just as important as antidiscrimination surrounding race, religion, and ethnic heritage. Nurse administrators must ensure that policies are put in place to prevent discrimination — both personally and professionally — toward any person merely because of gender or sexual orientation. Failure to do so erodes the very philosophical underpinning of the profession — caring — and severely hampers the potential human resources brought to the profession by both men and women, be they heterosexual, gay, or lesbian.

Summary of Issues

1. Gender stereotyping within nursing adversely affects the careers of both female and male nurses.

2. Men often experience sexual discrimination in nursing, which includes others frequently asking them to justify nursing as their career choice.

3. Nurses provide less care and inferior care to gay and lesbian patients than to other patients.

4. Homosexuality is probably equally as common within nursing as in the rest of society.

5. Homosexuals experience frequent harassment and should be recognized as a minority deserving legal protection of their civil rights.

Recommended Strategies

1. Stereotyping and sexism in the workplace must be acknowledged.

2. Mentoring programs to provide social support for men in nursing should be created.

3. A climate of support for sexual harassment sanctions in the workplace should be created.

4. Professional nursing organizations should become politically active in the support of legislation to protect the civil rights of homosexuals.

5. Gender issues should be addressed in graduate and undergraduate nursing curricula in relation to topics on professional matters, leadership, management, vulnerable populations, mental health, HIV/AIDS, and all other relevant course work.

6. Sexual orientation and sexuality should be included in cultural awareness and skill-based curricula in schools of nursing and continuing education.

Preferred Outcomes

1. The eradication of sexual stereotyping and its constraints on the power and practice of the nursing profession will occur.

2. Nurses will value men as equal colleagues in nursing.

3. The civil rights of gays and lesbians will become protected by law.

4. Nurses will value those with differing sexual orientations, and will be knowledgeable of the cultural meanings of sexuality.

5. Compassionate nursing care will be provided for patients with all sexual orientations.

References

American Nurses Association. 1978. American Nurses Association Resolution #51. Kansas City, Mo.: American Nurses Association.

Bem, S.L. 1974. The measurement of psychological androgyny. Journal of Consulting and Clinical Psychology 42 (2): 155-162.

———. 1977. On the utility of alternative procedures for assessing psychological androgyny. Journal of Consulting and Clinical Psychology 45 (2): 196-205.

———. 1981. Bem's sex-role inventory: Professional manual. Palo Alto, Calif.: Consulting Psychologist Press, Inc.

Borman, J.S. 1993. Chief nurse executives' balance of their work and personal lives. Nursing Administration Quarterly 18 (1): 30-39.

Bowler, I. 1993. They're not the same as us: Midwives' stereotypes of South Asian descent maternity patients. Social Health and Illness 15 (2): 157-178.

Brown, C.A. 1983. Women workers in the health service industry. In The politics of sex in medicine, ed. E. Fee, pp. 105-116. Farmingdale, N.Y.: Baywood.

Buchan, J. 1995. Male nurses: Losing their job advantage? Nursing Standard 9 (33): 30.

Bullough, V. 1993. Inquiry, insights, and history. History, nature, and nurture. Journal of Professional Nursing 9 (3): 128.

———. 1997. Men in nursing: Problems and perspectives. In Current issues in nursing, 5th ed., eds. J. McCloskey and H. Grace, pp. 589-594. St. Louis: Mosby.

Butter, I.H.; Carpenter, E.; Kay, B.J.; and Simmons, R. 1987. Gender hierarchies in the health labor force. Intervention: Journal of Human Services 17 (1): 133-149.

Christman, L.P. 1988a. Men in nursing. In Annual review of nursing research, vol. 6, eds. J. Fitzpatrick, R.L. Taunton, J.Q. Benoliel, pp. 193-205. Philadelphia: Springer. 1988b. Men in nursing. Imprint 35 (3): 75.

Cummings, S. 1995. Attila the Hun versus Attila the hen: Gender socialization of the American nurse. Nursing Administration Quarterly 19 (2): 19-29.

D'Augelli, A. 1989. Lesbians' and gay men's experiences of discrimination and harassment in a university community. American Journal of Community Psychology 17 (3): 317-321.

Deevey, S. 1993. Lesbian self-disclosure. Strategies for success. Journal of Psychosocial Nursing and Mental Health Services 31 (4): 21-26.

Dipboye, R.C. 1987. Problems and progress of women in management. In Working women: Past, present, future, eds. K.S. Koziara, M.H. Moskow, and L.D. Tanner, pp. 118-153. Washington, D.C.: BNA Books.

Douglas, C.J.; Kalman, C.M.; and Kalman, T.P. 1985. Homophobia among physicians and nurses: An empirical study. Hospital and Community Psychiatry 36 (12): 1309-1311.

Eakes, G. and Lewis, J. 1991. Should nurses be required to administer care to patients with AIDS? Students respond. Nurse Educator 16 (2): 36-38.

Edwards, J.B. and Lenz, C. 1990. The influence of gender on communications for nurse leaders. Nursing Administration Quarterly 15 (1): 49-55.

Egeland, J.W. and Brown, J.S. 1988. Sex role stereotyping and role strain of male registered nurses. Research in Nursing and Health 11: 257-267.

Fitzpatrick, J. and Whall, A. 1989. Conceptual models of nursing: Analysis and application. Norwalk, Conn.: Appleton & Lange.

Flint, C.; Turton, P.; Goodwin, S.; Bolger, T.; and Newberger, J. 1986. AIDS and the moral majority. Nursing Times, November 19, p. 22.

Freiberg, P. 1987. New report on hate crimes. The Advocate, December 22, pp. 10-11, 20.

Garnets, L. and D'Augelli, A. 1994. Empowering lesbian and gay communities: A call for collaboration with community psychology. American Journal of Community Psychology 22 (4): 447-470.

Gordon, S.I.; Herrick, C.A.; and Benvenutti, J.C. 1994. Gender differences in nursing. Imprint 41 (5): 47-49.

Greenhouse, L. 1986. High court, 5-4, says states have the right to outlaw private homosexual acts. New York Times, July 1, pp. 1, 19.

Habayeb, G.L. 1995. Cultural diversity: A nursing concept not yet reliably defined. Nursing Outlook 43 (5): 224-227.

Hall, B.A. 1993. Time to nurse: Musings of an aging nurse radical. Nursing Outlook 41 (6): 250-252.

Huerta, S. and Oddi, L. 1992. Refusal to care for patients with human immunodeficiency virus/acquired immunodeficiency syndrome: Issues and responses. Journal of Professional Nursing 8 (4): 221-230.

Kalisch, P. and Kalisch, B. 1986. The advance of American nursing, 2nd ed. Boston: Little Brown.

Keeter, M. 1994. Sex discrimination targets some men in hospitals. The American Nurse, April, pp. 3, 24.

Kerswell, J. and Booth, J. 1995. New degrees of prejudice. Nursing Standard 9 (4): 46.

Kim, J.H. and Perfect, J.R. 1988. To help the sick: A historical and ethical essay concerning the refusal to care for patients with AIDS. American Journal of Medicine 84 (1): 135- 138.

Kissick, W. 1966. Health manpower in transition. Washington, D.C.: U.S. Public Health Service.

Krasnik, A.; Fouchard, J.; Bayer, T.; and Keiding, N. 1990. Health workers and AIDS: Knowledge, attitudes, and experiences as determinants of anxiety. Scandinavian Journal of Social Medicine 18 (2): 103-113.

Krausz, M.; Kedem, P.; Tal, Z.; and Amir, Y. 1992. Sex role orientation and work adaptation of male nurses. Research in Nursing and Health 15: 391-398.

Lankewish, V. 1987. What rural America needs to know about AIDS. Healthlink, December, pp. 30-31.

Lewis, S. and Bor, R. 1994. Nurses' knowledge of and attitudes toward sexuality and the relationship of these with nursing practice. Journal of Advanced Nursing 20: 251-259.

Malone, B. 1997. Why isn't nursing more diversified? In Current issues in nursing, 5th ed., eds. J. McCloskey and H. Grace, pp. 574-579. St. Louis: Mosby.

Martindale, L. and Barnett, C. 1992. Nursing faculty's knowledge and attitudes toward persons with AIDS. Journal of the Association of Nurses in AIDS Care 3 (2): 9-13.

McCann, T. 1995. The global epidemic of human immunodeficiency virus infection: Past reflections, future directions. Holistic Nursing Practice 9 (2): 18-29.

McKenna, H.P. 1991. The developments and trends in relation to men practicing midwifery: A review of the literature. Journal of Advanced Nursing 16: 480-489.

Meisenhelder, J. 1994. Contributing factors to fear of HIV contagion in registered nurses. Image: The Journal of Nursing Scholarship 26 (1): 65-69.

Morrison, A.M. and von Glinow, M. 1990. Women and minorities in management. American Psychologist 45 (2): 200-208.

Moses, E. 1996. Unpublished data from the March 1996 National Sample Survey of Registered Nurses. Division of Nursing, Bureau of Health Professions, Health Research and Services Administration, Department of Health and Human Services, Rockville, Md.

Okrainec, G.D. 1994. Perceptions of nursing education held by male nursing students. Western Journal of Nursing Research 16 (1): 94-107.

Peate, I. 1995. A question of prejudice: Stigma, homosexuality, and HIV/AIDS. Professional Nurse 10 (6): 380-383.

Perkins, J.L.; Bennett, D.N.; and Dorman, R.E. 1993. Why men choose nursing. Nursing and Health Care 14 (1): 34-38.

Plasek, J. and Allard, J. 1984. Misconceptions of homophobia. Journal of Homosexuality 10 (1-2): 23-37.

Porter-O'Grady, T. 1995. Reverse discrimination in nursing leadership: Hitting the concrete ceiling. Nursing Administration Quarterly 19 (2): 56-62.

Powell, G.N. 1993. Women and men in management, 2nd ed. Newbury Park, Calif.: Sage.

Reed, P.; Wise, T.N.; and Mann, L.S. 1984. Nurses' attitudes regarding acquired immunodeficiency syndrome (AIDS). Nursing Forum 21 (4): 153-156.

Remafedi, G. 1987. Male homosexuality: The adolescent's perspective. Pediatrics 79 (3): 326- 330.

Rose, P. 1993. Out in the open? Nursing Times 89 (30): 50-52.

Ryan, S. and Porter, S. 1993. Men in nursing: A cautionary comparative critique. Nursing Outlook 41 (6): 262-267.

Sartorelli, J. 1994. Gay rights and affirmative action. Journal of Homosexuality 27 (3-4): 179-222.

Scherer, Y; Wu, R.; and Haughey, L. 1991. AIDS and homophobia among nurses. Journal of Homosexuality 21 (4): 17-27.

Schwanberg, S. 1990. Attitudes toward homosexuality in American health care literature. Journal of Homosexuality 19 (3): 117-136.

Sell, R.L.; Wells, J.A.; and Wypij, D. 1995. The prevalence of homosexual behavior and attraction in the United States, the United Kingdom, and France: Results of national population-based samples. Archives of Sexual Behavior 24 (3): 235-248.

Sherrod, R.A. 1991. Obstetrical role strain for male nursing students. Western Journal of Nursing Research 13 (4): 494-502.

Smith, G. 1992. Nursing care challenges: Homosexual psychiatric patients. Journal of Psychosocial Nursing and Mental Health Services 30 (12): 15-21.

Snavely, B.K. and Fairhurst, G. 1984. The male student as a token. Research in Nursing and Health 7: 287-294.

Sorofman, B. 1986. Research in cultural diversity: Defining diversity. Western Journal of Nursing Research 8 (1): 121-123.

Squires, T. 1995. Men in nursing. RN 58 (7): 26.

Steinbrook, R.; Lo, B.; Tirpack, J.; Dilley, J.W.; and Volberding, P.A. 1985. Ethical dilemmas in caring for patients with acquired immunodeficiency syndrome. Annals of Internal Medicine 103: 787-790.

Stevens, P. and Hall, J. 1991. A critical historical analysis of the medical construction of lesbianism. International Journal of Health Services 21 (2): 291-307.

Stivers, C. 1991. Why can't a woman be less like a man? Journal of Nursing Administration 21 (5): 47-51.

Streubert, H. 1994. Male nursing students' perceptions of clinical experience. Nurse Educator 19 (5): 28-32.

Taylor, I. and Robertson, A. 1994. The health needs of gay men: A discussion of the literature and implications for nursing. Journal of Advanced Nursing 20 (3): 560-566.

Williams, C.L., ed. 1993. Doing women's work: Men in nontraditional occupations. Newbury Park, Calif.: Sage.

_____. 1995. Hidden advantages for men in nursing. Nursing Administration Quarterly 19 (2): 63-70.

Young, E.W. 1988. Nurses' attitudes toward homosexuality: Analysis of change in AIDS workshops. Journal of Continuing Education in Nursing 19 (1): 9-12.

Young, M.; Henderson, M.; and Marx, D. 1990. Attitudes of nursing students toward patients with AIDS. Psychological Reports 67 (2): 491-496.

Zeidenstein, L. 1990. Gynecological and childbearing needs of lesbians. Journal of Nurse-Midwifery 35 (1): 10-18.

Chapter 4

Immigrant Nursing Personnel: The View from CGFNS

Catherine R. Davis, PhD, RN
Virginia M. Maroun, MSN, RN

The immigration of nurses into the United States has traditionally been viewed as both beneficial and problematic. Nurses educated outside the boundaries of the United States have provided relief during cyclical nursing shortages in this country and have helped increase awareness of the inherent value in cultural diversity. However, they also have been perceived as a factor in the decrease of available nursing positions in the United States when the labor market has been uncertain. The movement of nurses across international borders presents unlimited opportunities and challenges for immigrant nurses, American nurses, and U.S. health care institutions.

Background

Nurses educated outside the United States have been a presence in the U.S. work force since World War II, entering this country as either temporary workers or permanent residents (Yoder 1995). Changes in U.S. immigration laws in the late 1960s and early 1970s resulted in a steady increase in the number of nurses entering the United States as immigrants with preferred status because nurses were in short supply in this country. Although admitted on a temporary basis, these nurses routinely had their stays extended to the maximum amount of time permitted (Kalisch and Kalisch 1986).

The perception that U.S. health care providers were becoming increasingly dependent on temporary, foreign nurses and the concern among some labor organizations and U.S. workers that immigrant nurses might have a detrimental effect on the salaries and working conditions of the domestic work force led to the enactment of the Immigration Nursing Relief Act (INRA) of 1989. This law created the H-1A temporary nurse employment visa category for a five-year period; it allowed continued employer access to temporary foreign nurses, while decreasing dependence on that work force as quickly as possible. The law instituted stricter provisions for future nursing immigration, while attempting to avoid disruption of health care services throughout the United States by granting generous provisions for permanent resident status of registered nurses already in this country (Immigration Nursing Relief Advisory Committee 1995).

In the absence of any congressional action to extend or renew INRA, the law expired on August 31, 1995. Foreign nurses technically are eligible to enter the United States under the H-1B visa category; however, this may prove to be quite difficult. Nurses entering under an H-1B visa must demonstrate that they have earned the equivalent of a baccalaureate or higher degree, and prospective U.S. employers must demonstrate that the position to be filled requires an individual to have a minimum of a baccalaureate degree. Since there is no profession-wide standard of a baccalaureate degree for entry into practice, few immigrant nurses may qualify for this visa. The number of H-1B visas issued each year also is restricted. However, permanent occupational visas still may be obtained by registered nurses who, since passage of the 1990 Immigration Act, enter under the Third Preference, Schedule A. Occupations and professions listed on Schedule A are not required to have individual labor certifications since they have been predetermined by the U.S. Department of Labor to be in short supply in the United States.

Canadian and Mexican nurses are able to enter the United States under the Trade NAFTA (TN) visa. This visa category, created by the North American Free Trade Agreement (NAFTA), allows nurses from Canada and Mexico to enter the United States for an initial period of one year, which can be extended annually by the Immigration and Naturalization Service. There is no limit on the number of Canadians allowed admission under TN status. A cap is placed by NAFTA on the admission of all professionals (including RNs) from Mexico at 5,500 per year for the first 10 years of the agreement (Immigration Nursing Relief Advisory Committee 1995). However, NAFTA also mandates that this cap be eliminated by January 1, 2004. The Illegal Immigration Reform and Immigrant Responsibility Act of 1996 added a screening requirement for both temporary (including TN) and permanent nursing occupational visas. Nurses who are applying for visas must have a certificate issued by a credentials evaluation agency verifying that they have an education comparable to U.S. nursing education, a license that is valid and unencumbered, demonstrated proficiency in written and oral English, and passed the Commission on Graduates of Foreign Nursing Schools (CGFNS) Certification Examination or the National Council Licensure Examination (NCLEX-RN).

While concern has been raised that immigration programs jeopardize the livelihood of American nurses, it has been estimated that there were fewer than 14,000 H-1A nurses working in the United States at any given time during 1994. Factoring in nurses who entered the United States under TN visas in 1994 raises this number to approximately 21,000 nurses (Yoder and Feferman 1995). Based on these statistics, foreign-educated nurses represented only slightly more than one percent of the total U.S. nursing work force of approximately 2,000,000 registered nurses in 1994. While this is not a significant number, the challenges facing nurses who immigrate to the United States are significant and will be examined within the context of nursing education, regulation, and practice.

Education

Globalization is the integration of one nation's economy into the economies of many other nations (Jarratt et al. 1994). Today's society is undergoing rapid change due to the globalization not only of our economic institutions, but also of our intellectual and cultural institutions. Health care services and the education of health care professionals have not been immune to globalization.

The United States has the international distinction of hosting the largest number of foreign students studying outside their own countries. Included in this number are students looking to obtain basic and advanced degrees in nursing and students involved in time limited, nondegree-related educational experiences. Often, the primary goal of these educational efforts is the development of expert clinicians, researchers, administrators, and educators who can return to their home countries to expand the quality of nursing practice and education there (American Association of Colleges of Nursing 1994).

This situation creates a number of challenges, both for educational institutions and for nurses studying outside their own countries. One of the first issues that must be addressed involves the educational backgrounds that international nursing students bring to their U.S. educational endeavors. As in the United States, students in many other countries can enter into the nursing profession at the postsecondary level, primarily through diploma or baccalaureate programs. Unlike the United States, however, a number of countries throughout the world also offer nursing education at the secondary school level. Admission to such programs usually occurs after eight or nine years of primary and lower secondary school education, and at a time when the applicant may be only 14 years of age. These programs vary from country to country, are generally two to four years in length, and include compulsory general education courses, nursing courses, and noncompulsory electives. Faculty may comprise nurses, but are more likely to be general educators and physicians (Nursing in the World Editorial Committee 1993).

In the United States, basic nursing education programs prepare generalists, with specialization occurring at the graduate level. In other countries, basic nursing programs prepare not only first-level, general nurses, whose education is most comparable to that of a registered nurse in the United States, but also specialty nurses — e.g., psychiatric nurses, midwives, pediatric nurses, etc., whose programs do not include general nursing education (Nursing in the World Editorial Committee 1993). This diverse system of education can make it difficult for colleges or universities to appropriately determine the comparability of such programs to nursing programs in the United States, and to validate a nurse applicant's qualifications, knowledge, and skills. It also can lead to tremendous frustration on the part of the student who already has been recognized as a nurse in his or her own country.

A second challenge that presents itself to international students in the United States is adaptation to U.S. educational models and values. Pacquiao (1995) notes that the values of individualism, achievement orien-

tation, and self-reliance are fostered in nursing programs in the United States, and are considered essential to the assumption of professional nursing roles in this country. However, a lack of proficiency in the English language and contrasting cultural norms such as group-centeredness and mutual interdependence often place the international nursing student at a disadvantage in the American classroom. This clash of cultural values may contribute to an international nurse's sense of isolation, disillusionment, and decreased participation in the educational experience. This form of culture shock must be addressed if the educational experience is to be meaningful and valuable to all students.

A final challenge presents itself when international nursing students complete their educational objectives and return to their native countries. The return home requires another adjustment period that can create unanticipated stress. This type of stress, known as "reentry transition stress," develops more quickly and is often more severe and protracted than the culture shock experienced upon entry into a new country (Weaver 1994). The degree of reentry transition stress is directly proportional to the degree of adaptation to the host country — i.e., those who have adapted most easily to the host country have the most difficulty reentering their own culture. Few returnees and their families anticipate this period of adjustment, and fail to realize that they often view the world differently because of their experiences in another culture. Returnees may be envied within their own cultures, may have established different communication patterns, and may view the world through a more global perspective, yet they often are expected to be the same person on return as when they left. This can lead to depression, withdrawal, and decreased effectiveness. It also can interfere with the transfer of knowledge and technology that was expected to occur upon return, an especially problematic issue if returnees were sent by their governments to gain knowledge and skills that would enhance the development of nursing in their own countries (Weaver 1994).

All of these challenges raise questions regarding the broader picture of international nursing education and the movement of nurses across borders. If minimum educational standards vary from country to country, how will this affect the movement of nurses worldwide? Some countries are just beginning to move away from nursing at the secondary school level, while others are at the stage of requiring the baccalaureate degree as a minimum requirement for entry into practice. Given these continued differences, how can the standardization of nursing education among countries occur?

Although international cooperation and international education for health care personnel are challenged by conceptual and regulatory boundaries, several organizations (including the Center for Quality Assurance in International Education, the International Council for Nurses, Sigma Theta Tau, and CGFNS) are attempting to promote an international harmonization of standards for nursing and health care education. Centered around developing common standards for quality and increasing the accessibility of curricula and course programs to international students, such cooperative efforts can be expected to foster educational innovation and exchange. Academic recognition, credit transfer, program evaluation and improvement, and joint research are the essential common activities. Collaborative efforts are expected to lead to mutual recognition of educational programs, joint development and dissemination of new programs, increased mobility of faculty and students, elimination of existing barriers to cooperation, and development of joint programs in education,

evaluation, and research (Consortium of Institutes of Higher Education in Health and Rehabilitation in Europe 1995).

Regulation

The practice of licensing nurses in the United States began in the early 1900s (Kalisch and Kalisch 1986). Although all states use the same national licensing examination, each state establishes its own requirements for licensure and defines its own scope of practice for registered nurses. The licensure of foreign-educated nurses also is determined by each individual state (Yoder 1995).

Graduates of nursing schools located outside the United States must meet state licensure requirements and must obtain a license before being able to practice in this country. Historically, passing the U.S. licensure examination (NCLEX-RN) was problematic for foreign-educated nurses. In the mid-1970s, only 20 percent of foreign-educated nurses who entered the United States passed the licensure examination. Many of those who failed the NCLEX-RN had entered this country on temporary work visas that limited the length of their stays. As unlicensed nurses, they often were unable to secure employment and left the United States when their visas expired. Those who remained found employment as unlicensed nursing personnel with lower salaries, or were hired illegally as registered nurses, despite the fact that this often placed patients at great risk (U.S. Department of Health, Education, and Welfare 1976).

In 1977, in an effort to remedy this situation, the American Nurses Association (ANA), the National League for Nursing (NLN), the U.S. Department of Labor, and the Immigration and Naturalization Service (INS) jointly established CGFNS, a nonprofit organization responsible for the testing and evaluation of nurses educated outside the United States. The CGFNS certification program gives nurses who wish to immigrate to the United States an opportunity to know whether or not they have a reasonable chance of passing the U.S. licensure examination before they leave their home countries. Those educated as first-level general nurses (RNs) are eligible to sit for the CGFNS qualifying examination, which is administered worldwide. The examination is taken in two parts — an English portion, which measures vocabulary, basic principles of grammar, and listening comprehension; and a nursing portion. Once foreign nurses successfully complete both portions, they earn a certificate required for a work visa as a nurse. Present changes in immigration laws for nurses, however, have greatly reduced demand for this program.

This testing program helped to standardize the protocol for the entry of foreign nurses into the United States on a work visa, and provided an objective, predictive test for their success on the NCLEX-RN. The program also allowed nurses to assess their chances of being licensed in the United States without having to travel to this country, and helped to curb the abuses of foreign-educated nurses who were unable to pass the U.S. licensure examination.

Validity studies, conducted annually by CGFNS, have traditionally shown that 70 to 75 percent of foreign-educated nurses who pass the CGFNS qualifying examination on the first try also pass the NCLEX-RN on the first attempt. The 1994-95 CGFNS Validity Study, which examined the performance of CGFNS certificate holders on the NCLEX-RN from April 1994 through March 1995, showed an increase in the initial overall pass rate to 89.7 percent. Those who were unsuccessful on the CGFNS qualifying examination, but who took the NCLEX-RN in a state that did not require CGFNS, had a 39.4 percent

pass rate (Commission on Graduates of Foreign Nursing Schools 1996).

The international mobility of nurses is often challenging due to varying, inconsistent, and sometimes conflicting nursing regulations and practices. In some countries, nursing graduates may begin practice after successfully passing a national licensure examination, while in other countries, the school diploma gives legal entry into the profession. In still other countries, licensure is not granted until a period of service has been completed (Nursing in the World Editorial Committee 1993). As trade relations between nations are being redefined and the economies of nations are becoming increasingly intertwined, nursing must examine how it can promote the free movement of its professionals among nations.

The North American Free Trade Agreement is based on the principle of nondiscriminatory treatment. It eliminates citizenship and permanent residency requirements for North American nurses who wish to practice in one of the countries involved in the treaty (Canada, Mexico, and the United States). It provides for procedures to review nursing qualifications and promotes mutual recognition based on objective criteria. At the state level, no regulatory changes are prescribed by NAFTA other than the dissolution of citizenship and residency requirements. However, the practice of licensed professionals still requires compliance with all applicable state regulations (Trilateral Initiative for North American Nursing 1996). How can nursing best respond to the challenges and opportunities created by NAFTA?

The Trilateral Initiative for North American Nursing, supported by a grant from the W.K. Kellogg Foundation and coordinated by CGFNS, is a multilateral effort by nursing organizations in Canada, Mexico, and the United States to develop commonly accepted standards among the three countries for nursing education, program approval and accreditation, licensure and registration, and professional certification. Core groups, with members from each country, developed an important first tool — a comprehensive description of each country's current standards. Country-specific teams within each core group worked to systematically assess these standards. These findings have been merged into a single document that provides the first clear picture of how the three countries conduct nursing education, approve and accredit education programs, manage licensure and registration, and carry out certification (Trilateral Initiative for North American Nursing 1996).

Participants in the initiative were drawn from more than 35 groups, including professional nursing associations, educational institutions, and regulatory and policy-making agencies from all three countries. The initiative represents the first organized effort by health care professions to identify and examine the challenges and opportunities presented by NAFTA, and to craft a forward-looking response.

Practice

Nurses educated outside the United States generally require a period of acculturation to U.S. health care settings. After the traditional "honeymoon phase," the reality of living and working in a new culture takes hold and often can lead to disillusionment. Interpersonal communication begins to appear ineffective and often breaks down. Cut off from their support systems, immigrant nurses may long for the familiar and doubt their ability to solve problems and to function successfully in the new environment. The greater the difference in cultures, the greater the difficulty experienced during this period (Weaver 1994).

In a new culture, immigrants are more aware of what makes them different and consciously examine culturally embedded values, beliefs, and thought patterns. Values and behaviors reinforced at home often go unrewarded, and ways of perceiving reality and solving problems at home may not work in the new culture. In fact, immigrant nurses may be ascribed an entirely different role and status in the new culture from that to which they were accustomed at home. This frequently contributes to the culture shock experienced by many nurses who immigrate to the United States. The depression and learned helplessness that accompany this phenomenon may inhibit nurses' effectiveness and interfere with practice. Nurses who immigrate to the United States eventually develop a bicultural personality, which enables them to better adapt to the new culture (Weaver 1994).

Historically, the majority of nurses immigrating to the United States have been employed in hospital settings, particularly in urban areas, and have been paid salaries similar to U.S.-educated nurses. When they are paid on a higher scale, it is usually because they enter the U.S. work force with greater experience. The impact of foreign nurses on patient care has generally been positive. However, concern is sometimes raised about communication difficulties if English is not their native language. Communication difficulties have been noted with patients, families, and physicians, and occur most frequently during telephone conversations (Yoder and Feferman 1995).

The future of health care in the United States is uncertain as we move from hospital-based to community-based care, participate in managed care, and are involved in work redesign. The number of nurses primarily employed in hospital settings has been decreasing, and for the first time in recent history nurses have been faced with layoffs (Yoder 1995). It is unlikely that these changes will be reversed in the near future, and it remains unclear if the shift to community-based care will be able to sustain the American work force. What this means for the foreign-educated nurse also is unclear.

While foreign-educated nurses traditionally are employed in hospital settings, the move to community-based care may, in fact, be advantageous. The Healthy Cities/Healthy Communities initiative, with its focus on health as the pursuit of wellness, opens opportunities for the United States and other Western nations to apply "some of the lessons learned from the experiences of developing nations, which by necessity have been driven to adopt community development approaches to meeting health needs" (Smith 1995, p. 190). The practice of nursing in the United States may indeed benefit not only from the cultural diversity that the immigrant nurse brings to the practice setting, but also from the education and experience immigrant nurses bring to community-based nursing.

Collaborating for Change

In order to minimize the challenges facing nurses who immigrate to the United States and to ease their transition into this country, common ground must be achieved through collaborative efforts involving nursing education, regulation, and practice. Education must demystify the global trends that affect nursing practice in the United States. If students are made aware of the effects of globalization as they move through their educational programs, they will carry their awareness of the global arena into practice. As regulatory bodies see changes occurring in the global arena, they need to make the educational community and the practice sector aware of those changes and their potential effects on nursing.

Educational institutions must consider the special needs of international students. Support programs that address the acculturation process and focus on the culture and customs of the host town or city, in addition to those of the individual institution, may facilitate the transition of international students into U.S. colleges and universities. Forums at which international nursing students have opportunities to discuss health care practices and health care delivery within the context of their own cultures, and to compare and contrast their native health care systems to those in the United States, should be made an integral part of nursing programs. It also is vital that nursing curricula formally address reentry issues. Since most international students do not recognize the challenge of reentry into their own cultures (Weaver 1994), regular seminars should be conducted that include discussion of the personal, social, and professional expectations of returning students.

Leininger (1994) notes that educational institutions must develop a global focus in order to assist students of different cultures to function in a multicultural world. Faculty development programs should encourage faculty to explore not only transcultural nursing, but also their own cultural values, their beliefs about cultural diversity and cultural competence, and the effect their perceptions about multiculturalism have on the way in which they educate their students. Such knowledge is vital for faculty involved in the educational experiences of international nursing students.

Education and practice must take an active and collaborative role in recognizing the value of different cultures through formal and continuing education. Nursing has a richness and continuity that takes it beyond international borders, yet few nurses are aware of the nursing traditions embedded in cultures other than their own. Continuing education that addresses regulatory, education, and practice issues from an international perspective can help to expand the views of nurses in the United States and promote an awareness of the issues facing nursing in the global arena. At a more basic level, courses and conferences that examine the cultural and nursing practices of different communities, especially the cultures of those within the class, conference, or work setting, can help nurses to increase their knowledge of cultural similarities and differences and can promote nursing practice based on cultural awareness. These programs can offer nurses an opportunity to search for alternative solutions to patient-specific problems within a supportive group setting that promotes the collaboration and dialogue necessary for culturally sensitive practice.

Bernstein (1983) maintains that shared human vision drives people in their tasks. If a shared vision for nursing is international mobility and collaboration, regulatory changes must take into consideration the international nursing community. The report Critical Challenges: Revitalizing the Health Professions for the Twenty-First Century (Pew Health Professions Commission 1995) encourages standardization of the language of professional regulation, proposes the development of partnerships to streamline regulatory structures and processes, and recommends policies that facilitate professional and geographic mobility among competent health care providers. Mobility is the global future. However, the variance among nations in nursing education, professional qualification, and standards of practice hinders the movement of nurses across borders. Countries must collaborate and pool resources in order to establish international methods for assessing qualifications and equivalence of education; they must inform each other about their regulatory systems and processes; and they must exchange ideas, concerns, and expertise.

Conclusion

If nursing is going to achieve globalization, we need to expand our vision. This can only be done through collaboration. International borders are falling and nurses in the United States no longer can expect to practice in isolation. We need to recognize the importance of multicultural nursing in a pluralistic society and the responsibility that we, as nurses, have to our colleagues who come from outside the United States.

Trade agreements that provide for the movement of goods and services between countries provide unprecedented opportunities for nursing. Since they require the development of mutually acceptable standards among nations, we must have nurses at the table when trade agreements are made, and must have a vision for how these agreements can be implemented within the international nursing community. Common standards are vital if we are to protect the consumers of our services and maintain professional integrity.

Nurses must be aware of the actual and potential effects that trade reduction and the elimination of trade barriers may have on their practice. We must have the vision to manage for ourselves the changes necessitated by trade agreements, or someone else will do it for us. Most nurses are aware of the impact on practice of a slowing domestic economy. The major powers that dominate the world marketplace — the leading developers and users of technology — recognize that when the domestic economy slows, increased international partnerships lead to growth. Managed care, the trend toward community-based health care, the emergence of hospitals as acute care centers, the resulting shifts in positions for American nurses, and the increasing role of the insurance industry in the practice of nursing are reflective of the growing changes in U.S. health care.

Nursing also needs to develop a greater understanding of the global economy and how it affects nursing. Use of the Internet and video conferencing offer multiple opportunities for international education and practice. Nursing must continue to harness technology that facilitates international collaboration and communication and that informs nurses of international opportunities.

Promoting the nursing profession across borders and oceans is difficult work. Collaborating with colleagues so separated by distance, language, and culture presents many challenges, and is sometimes disruptive. However, the effort to form alliances where none existed before enables nursing to broaden its perspective and expand its vision at a time when change offers our profession unprecedented opportunity.

Summary of Issues

1. Globalization of the nation's economy, as well as of health care and educational institutions, is rapidly occurring. However, the majority of nurses and nursing institutions are unaware of its implications for the nursing profession.

2. The lack of global educational standards limits the international mobility of nurses.

3. There is no consistent and comprehensive policy regarding the immigration of nurses into the United States, even for temporary employment.

4. Compared to other disciplines, there are few joint educational, research, or student exchange programs between U.S. schools of nursing and foreign schools or between U.S. health services agencies and foreign agencies.

5. Requirements within the United States for licensure of foreign nursing graduates varies by state.

6. Nurses currently are not members of commissions drafting international agreements that affect the mobility of nurses for education and practice.

Recommended Strategies

1. Entry and continuing education programs for nurses will include trends in globalization, cultural sensitivity, and foreign nursing traditions in their curricula.

2. Schools of nursing in the United States that accept international students will develop student services to assist in adjustment to American teaching methods and values, in improvement of English language skills, in awareness of American and foreign cultures for students and faculty, and in preparation for culture shock upon students' return home.

3. The Commission on Graduates of Foreign Nursing Schools, in collaboration with the American Association of Colleges of Nursing, will continue to develop a country-by-country comparability index for educational assessment and requirements for the articulation of nurses wishing to further their education through international study.

4. Schools of nursing, academic health centers, managed care organizations, and state health departments will seek joint ventures and programs for nursing education, research, and practice improvement with international governments and organizations.

5. The National Council of State Boards of Nursing will provide leadership in streamlining professional regulation regarding the licensure of foreign nurses.

6. The Division of Nursing of the U.S. Department of Health and Human Services and organizations such as CGFNS and the American Academy of Nursing will provide leadership in seeking nurse representation on commissions that create trade agreements affecting nurse mobility.

Preferred Outcomes

1. The standards for nursing education, accreditation, registration, licensure, and certification developed between the United States, Canada, and Mexico by the Trilateral Initiative for North American Nursing will become a model for global collaboration on nursing eduction and practice.

2. Nurses in the United States will not see controlled immigration of foreign nurses as a threat to their careers.

3. Nurses from all countries will be able to temporarily practice in the United States for both educational purposes and career enhancement under a specific visa.

4. Employers of nurses in the United States will view international experience as a career advantage in selection and recruitment.

5. National standards and protocols for the international educational mobility of nurses will be developed and utilized by U.S. schools of nursing.

6. Schools of nursing in the United States will facilitate study, research, and joint program development with international schools, students, and scholars.

7. Private and public health services agencies and managed care organizations will seek nursing exchanges and collaborative projects for program evaluation and improvement, continuing education, research, management, practice, and standards of practice.

8. Nurses will become members of trade commissions that develop regulations affecting nurse mobility and education.

References

American Association of Colleges of Nursing. 1994. Licensure of international students. Position statement, Washington, D.C.

Bernstein, R. 1983. Beyond objectivism and relativism: Science, hermeneutics, and praxis. Philadelphia: University of Pennsylvania Press.

Commission on Graduates of Foreign Nursing Schools. 1996. Validity study on CGFNS qualifying examinations as predictors of success on NCLEX-RN, April 1994 through March 1995, Philadelphia.

Consortium of Institutes of Higher Education in Health and Rehabilitation in Europe. 1995. Report of study visit to U.S.A. and Canada, Nijmegen, Netherlands.

Immigration Nursing Relief Advisory Committee, ed. 1995. Report to the Secretary of Labor on the Immigration Nursing Relief Act of 1989. Washington, D.C.: U.S. Government Printing Office.

Jarratt, J.; Coates, J.; Mahaffie, J.; and Hines, A. 1994. Managing your future as an association. Washington, D.C.: American Society of Association Executives Foundation.

Kalisch, P. and Kalisch, B. 1986. The advance of American nursing, 2nd ed. Boston: Little Brown.

Leininger, M. 1994. Transcultural nursing education: A worldwide imperative. Nursing and Health Care 15 (5): 254-257.

Nursing in the World Editorial Committee, International Nursing Foundation of Japan, ed. 1993. Nursing in the world: Facts, needs, and prospects, 3rd ed. Tokyo: International Nursing Foundation of Japan.

Pacquiao, D.F. 1995. Multicultural issues in nursing practice and education. Issues: A Newsletter of the National Council 16 (2): 1, 4-5, 11.

Pew Health Professions Commission. 1995. Critical challenges: Revitalizing the health professions for the twenty-first century, 3rd report. Philadelphia: Pew Health Professions Commission.

Smith, G.R. 1995. Lessons learned: Challenges for the future. Nursing and Health Care 16 (4): 188-191.

Trilateral Initiative for North American Nursing. 1996. An assessment of North American nursing. Philadelphia: Commission on Graduates of Foreign Nursing Schools.

U.S. Department of Health, Education, and Welfare. 1976. Survey of foreign nurse graduates. Washington, D.C.: U.S. Government Printing Office.

Weaver, G. 1994. The process of reentry. The Advising Quarterly (27): 1, 3-8.

Yoder, S.G. 1995. Registered nurses in the United States. In Report to the Secretary of Labor on the Immigration Nursing Relief Act of 1989, ed. Immigration Nursing Relief Advisory Committee, F43-55. Washington, D.C.: U.S. Government Printing Office.

Yoder, S.G. and Feferman, F. 1995. How many H-1A nurses? In Report to the Secretary of Labor on the Immigration Nursing Relief Act of 1989, ed. Immigration Nursing Relief Advisory Committee, F29-42. Washington, D.C.: U.S. Government Printing Office.

Chapter 5
Hispanic Immigrant Nursing Personnel: A Cultural Exemplar

Helen M. Castillo, PhD, RN, FAAN

Historically, nurses have been recruited from local populations that are predominantly white and English-speaking. Traditionally, individuals from different countries, different ethnicities, or who speak English as a second language have been negatively characterized by health care agencies as less desirable for nursing positions, for reasons including language difficulties and cultural differences from client populations (Malone 1997; Brink 1990). Such characterizations are no longer valid — if they ever were. By recognizing that the United States today is a multiculturally diverse and heterogenous country, one realizes that immigrants and ethnic minorities need to be viewed as personnel resources, not liabilities.

In considering the makeup of various minority populations, one need only review demographic data to learn that Hispanics[0] comprise the fastest growing and youngest U.S. minority population, followed by Asians (U.S. News and World Report 1995). All Hispanics are not alike, however; they vary in national origin, cultural practices, religious beliefs, socioeconomic status, and acculturation levels. The culture and customs of Mexico, for example, are different from those of Cuba, Puerto Rico, Guatemala, San Salvador, Brazil, and Chile, and individuals from each country speak a distinct form of Spanish (with the exception of Brazilians, who speak Portuguese).

Non-Europeans, considered ethnic minorities in the past, are fast becoming an aggregate majority, and specific groups are becoming ethnic majorities in selected parts of the United States. Hispanics living in Los Angeles, San Antonio, and Miami, for example, now make up the majority population in their communities. Other cities of similar size are gaining momentum in changing their ethnic demographic compositions (U.S. Public Health Service 1992).

Immigrants as Nursing Personnel

Until the late 1960s and early 1970s, the option of recruiting qualified immigrants as nurses was not pursued by many hospitals. Then, in response to a severe nursing shortage in the mid-1980s, multiple hiring agencies sprang forward and found the recruitment of foreign nurses to be a financial windfall. State boards of nursing responded to the increased hiring of foreign nurses by enforcing stringent requirements on the hiring practices of employing agencies and by tightening the licensure requirements for foreign graduates. At the same time, hospitals often exploited foreign nurses by hiring them for undesirable work assignments at reduced salaries, and by enforcing legally questionable work contracts. Upon completing a contract, most foreign nurses returned to their countries of origin (Immigration Nursing Relief Advisory Committee 1995).

Today, qualified professional nurses and other specialized health care personnel of immigrant status need to be selected based on specific community and regional needs. One such need might include the existence of large numbers of Hispanic residents in certain communities, along with a severe shortage of health care professionals who understand the Spanish language and Hispanic cultures. The recruitment of Hispanic foreign nurses will need to include a multifaceted approach that matches the needs of the community, the health care system, and the nurse recruits. Additionally, health care providers must be closely monitored to avoid employment saturations of selected types of personnel and new reductions in the U.S. work force.

The Need for Hispanic Nurses

Southwest border communities, in particular, face problems of binational and bicultural health care needs, which continue to increase in magnitude and complexity. These geographic areas are prime examples of the need for more Hispanic nursing personnel to provide culturally competent health care. Most graduates of American nursing programs do not speak Spanish, are not educated in Hispanic health beliefs and practices or the differences among various Hispanic groups, and often are nonresponsive to recruitment efforts to serve these populations (Torres and Castillo 1997). Unrecognized until recently, this need for Hispanic nurses is expected to rapidly expand in large cities such as Chicago and New York where Hispanics are fast becoming ethnic majorities (U.S. Census Bureau 1993).

In the past, the activities and health care needs of border countries were not important to most U.S. citizens unless they had a direct impact on national affairs. This view is fast changing, with an emerging global perspective influenced by increasing international trade, multinational corporations and careers, and trends in immigration patterns. This increasingly global perspective is already affecting policies in the United States and will continue to further influence all aspects of our society.

International recruitment is one option for hiring qualified nurses to fill continuing vacant or multiple anticipated positions in Hispanic communities. Foreign Hispanic nurses continue to seek the challenges, unique professional growth opportunities, and salaries provided within the U.S. health

care system. Since most nursing education programs in Spanish-speaking countries are not at the baccalaureate level, these nurses might seek opportunities for future advancement at U.S. colleges and universities, where they can contribute to the cultural diversity of the nursing student populations of RN-BSN and higher degree programs.

Along with demographic changes, major reforms taking place in the U.S. health care system dictate the need for a more open, community-based approach to health care. Requirements for innovative community-based programs to promote health and provide quality care within ethnic communities will demand increased cultural knowledge and bilingual fluency. The development of such programs will be best accomplished by enlisting the energies of immigrant and American-born Hispanic and other ethnic practitioners, educators, and administrators.

Critics of such efforts might believe that immigrants, professionally prepared or not, should remain in their own countries, especially when a great number of U.S. citizens have experienced the effects of layoffs, downsizings, and other business cutbacks. The same critics might say that these citizens are the appropriate candidates to prepare to meet our nation's changing health care needs. In fact, however, when the characteristics of the unemployed or underemployed are assessed, a large number of Hispanic Americans is found. In 1990, for example, 27 percent of Hispanic families lived below the poverty level, compared to 10 percent of non-Hispanic families (U.S. Census Bureau 1993). This population represents another source for recruiting Hispanic nursing personnel, albeit one that requires specialized recruitment and educational efforts.

Yet another source for recruiting more Hispanic nurses includes foreign graduates of U.S. schools of nursing. An increasing number of international immigrants are attending universities across the United States. Upon graduation, many of these foreign graduates desire to remain in this country to practice their new skills and knowledge; this is especially true of physicians and nurses and, in selected universities, geologists and engineers (American Association of Colleges of Nursing 1994). These university-educated immigrant nursing personnel from Hispanic countries could become an important resource in focused recruitment efforts.

The Demands of Border Corporations

For more than 10 years, the "twin plant model" of industry (Ganster 1987; State National Bank of El Paso 1974) has included the hiring of immigrants or the transferring of employees to become immigrants from both sides of the U.S.-Mexico border by major corporations, such as Coca-Cola and IBM (Solunet 1991). These plants are bilingual and hire employees at all levels from both countries. Additional corporations — based primarily in Mexico, with satellite offices in Arizona, California, New Mexico, and Texas — are beginning to expand beyond the border states to other cities with substantial Hispanic populations as they identify Hispanic Americans as a market niche. American-born and Mexican-born employees hired for corporate management positions in these companies must be fluent in the languages, cultures, and customs of both countries, and must be willing to have binational careers (Kelly, Whatley, and Zarate 1989; Kras 1989; George and Tollen 1983). Partially due to the North American Free Trade Agreement (NAFTA), several for-profit health care corporations operating in the border states have recently adopted the twin plant model, thereby increasing employment opportunities for bicultural and bilingual nurses from Mexico and the United States. Additionally,

according to Jacqueline Agnew (1997), head of occupational health nursing at The Johns Hopkins University, international corporations located in the United States, Mexico, Central America, and South America also are recruiting professional occupational health nurses who are bilingual and bicultural to work with their multicultural employee populations.

As changes in manufacturing and other industries result from NAFTA and other trade agreements, nursing must be alert for the impact of such trade agreements on health care delivery and the health of workers in NAFTA countries. NAFTA currently requires monitoring of the number of professional immigrants allowed to enter this country, including registered nurses, physicians, and other professional health care providers; state boards of nursing should pay particularly close attention (Immigration Nursing Relief Advisory Committee 1995). Consumers do cross borders to exercise choices regarding alternative medicine, the cost and quality of specific procedures, and the cultural competence of providers. One effect of NAFTA is the increased hiring of immigrant personnel across both the U.S. and Mexican borders. Another related effect is increased interaction between schools of nursing and health care agencies in U.S. border states and Mexico. Some schools of nursing are now offering clinical experiences in Mexico as a learning option to improve students' Spanish language skills and cultural competence. Bilingualism, biculturalism, and other proactive global skills are becoming recognized as valuable assets by employers (Ganster 1987). The full impact of NAFTA on health care issues between the United States and Mexico, however, probably will not be realized for another 10 to 15 years.

The Demands of Consumers

Globally, health care models are moving toward integrated care delivery across the life span. With the advent of managed care and prepaid health care in the United States, there is more concern about costs and profits. Primary care is thus emerging as the mode for continuity of care and maintenance of consumers' health. This shift from an emphasis on technology for disease care to an emphasis on primary care moves control over health care from the provider alone to control jointly shared with the consumer. Health care providers must work with consumers to examine practices and beliefs in relation to health status in order to redefine appropriate care. Such a redefinition must include the expectations by bilingual and bicultural consumers that their health care providers also will be bilingual and bicultural. As an essential skill, the cultural competence of health care providers has risen to the foreground.

Increasing cultural diversity is a significant element in health care today, from both provider and consumer viewpoints. Providers are still expected to provide quality care to culturally diverse groups regardless of race, color, or creed, including ethnic origin, cultural values, social values, and other perceived differences between provider and consumer. On one hand, health care consumers expect culturally sensitive care based on their personal needs and expectations. On the other hand, health care providers expect consumers to be knowledgeable about standards of care developed for primarily western European, English-speaking, college-educated, middle-class Americans (Andrews and Boyle 1995). These differing expectations act as communication barriers that can result in serious misunderstandings or conflict between the health care provider and consumer. It follows that health care personnel need to ask themselves two basic questions: (1) "Whose responsibility is it to provide quality care?" and (2) "What are the essential elements of that care?" Answers to these questions point out that blaming a low quality of care on ethnic consumers' lack of comprehension of the English language and American health care practices is no longer acceptable.

Consumers are making new demands for cultural competence in health care at a time when specific cultural knowledge about immigrant groups often is still limited or nonexistent.

Culturally competent and culturally sensitive health care will be realized through nursing position qualifications requiring cultural competency and fluency in the language and health practices of dominant client populations, and by schools of nursing including language requirements and modeling the importance of cultural competence on quality health care provision.

Under such cultural competency requirements, immigrant Hispanic nursing personnel may have an advantage in seeking positions that involve caring for substantial numbers of Hispanic clients. Immigrant Hispanic nursing personnel also may act as key information sources for their peers regarding the nuances of communication and the immigrant perspective, and can provide the essential psychosocial and health care support that minority communities often must do without.

Conclusion

Until cultural competence and cultural sensitivity ideals are reached, employers providing care to substantial numbers of Hispanic clients should state a hiring preference for bilingual and bicultural nurses. For current non-Hispanic nurses, employers should provide access to mandatory classes in basic Spanish and in Hispanic cultures and customs. Since many nurses may need to be convinced of the positive impact this will have on their practice, employers should provide incentives for training, such as offering courses at the work site and during paid working hours. Such incentives should be phased in with performance requirements for course achievement within certain time periods.

Knowledge of the Spanish language and Hispanic cultural practices is a prerequisite for even adequate nursing care of Hispanic clients. For example, speaking the Spanish language enables nurses to identify relevant patient experiences and health care practices that affect the quality of care provided to Hispanics. A key ingredient to open information sharing is trust, which does not develop between health care workers and their Hispanic patients if the worker lacks at least a basic knowledge of the Spanish language. Without open dialogue and information sharing, vital health care information may be missed, compliance may be impaired, and future health care needs may not be identified. Without this type of knowledge, quality health care is clearly unattainable for Hispanics and other immigrant groups.

Summary of Issues

1. Traditional nursing hiring practices favor Americans of western European backgrounds.

2. Immigrants and Americans speaking English as a second language face prejudice, racism, lack of career mobility, and a higher likelihood of undesirable work assignments in nursing careers.

3. Homogeneity of the nursing work force does not reflect the cultural mix of our country, especially the states bordering Mexico. This is a significant barrier to culturally competent care.

4. Hispanics and other minority patients too often do not receive culturally appropriate care.

5. NAFTA is creating increased opportunities for Mexican and Canadian nurses to practice in the United States.

Recommended Strategies

1. International nursing organizations will work to establish standards of education that will facilitate the mobility of nurses across national boundaries.

2. American nursing organizations will actively seek to have NAFTA lift the quota for Mexican health care personnel, while maintaining the same high standards for nurse registration reciprocity.

3. Schools of nursing will require a second language of all students. Faculty will be expected to progressively increase their cultural knowledge and grasp of a second language.

4. Schools of nursing will examine their student recruitment activities to identify how to attract more Hispanic American students and foreign Hispanic students.

5. Nurse administrators will review and revise hiring and job placement policies and practices to enhance the valuing of immigrant nurses and eradicate exploitation.

6. Health care organizations will include the utilization of cultural brokering as a performance expectation among nursing personnel.

Preferred Outcomes

1. The cultural mix of a locality will be reflected in the cultural mix of health care providers and managers.

2. Immigrant nurses will be valued as cultural brokers and interpreters for patients and for other health care personnel.

3. Health care organizations in cities with majority Hispanic populations will require cultural competence of all employees, including a progressive knowledge of Spanish, Mexican, and Latin American cultures, health beliefs, and practices.

4. Job exploitation of immigrant nurses will cease.

5. Patients will have access to culturally competent care that incorporates both Western medicine and health care practices consistent with their own worldviews.

References

Agnew, J. Conversation with J. Dienemann, Baltimore, Md., June 1, 1997.

American Association of Colleges of Nursing. 1994. Licensure of international students. Position statement, Washington, D.C.

Andrews, M.M. and Boyle, J.S. 1995. Transcultural concepts in nursing care, 2nd ed. Philadelphia: J.B. Lippincott.

Brink, P. 1990. Cultural diversity in nursing: How much can we tolerate? In Current issues in nursing, 4th ed., eds. J. McCloskey and H. Grace, pp. 658-664. St. Louis: Mosby.

Ganster, P., ed. 1987. The maquiladora program in tri-national perspective: Mexico, Japan, and the United States. San Diego, Calif.: San Diego State University, Institute for Regional Studies of the Californias.

George, E.Y. and Tollen, R.D. 1983. The economic impact of the Mexican border industrialization program. El Paso, Texas: The University of Texas at El Paso, Center for Inter-American Border Studies.

Immigration Nursing Relief Advisory Committee, ed. 1995. Report to the Secretary of Labor on the Immigration Nursing Relief Act of 1989. Washington, D.C.: U.S. Government Printing Office.

Kelly, N.L.; Whatley, A.; and Zarate, N. 1989. Managing in Mexico: A cultural perspective. Las Cruces, N.M.: New Mexico State University, Joint Border Research Institute.

Kras, E.S. 1989. Management in two cultures: Bridging the gap between U.S. and Mexican managers. Yarmouth, Maine: Intercultural Press.

Malone, B. 1997. Why isn't nursing more diversified? In Current issues in nursing, 5th ed., eds. J. McCloskey and H. Grace, pp. 574-579. St. Louis: Mosby.

Solunet. 1991. The complete twin plant guide. El Paso, Texas: Solunet.

State National Bank of El Paso, International Banking and Industrial Development Department. 1974. The Mexican border industrialization program: "Twin plant" concept. El Paso, Texas: State National Bank of El Paso, International Banking and Industrial Development Department.

Torres, S. and Castillo, H. 1997. Bridging cultures: Hispanics/Latinos and nursing. In Current issues in nursing, 5th ed., eds. J. McCloskey and H. Grace, pp. 603-608. St. Louis: Mosby.

U.S. Census Bureau. 1993. Current population reports. Washington, D.C.: U.S. Government Printing Office.

U.S. News and World Report. 1995. Ahead: A mostly minority America. October 30, p. 23.

U.S. Public Health Service. 1992. U.S. census data, 1990. Washington, D.C.: U.S. Government Printing Office.

---

[o] The term "Hispanics" is used in this chapter as a synonym for Latinos and Latinas.

Chapter 6
Managing Intercultural Business Encounters[0]

Barbara J. Brown, EdD, RN, CNAA, FAAN, FNAP

Managing business encounters in an intercultural foreign health care setting requires considerable patience, adaptation, flexibility, innovation, creativity, openness, and willingness to develop collegial relationships with people holding a variety of worldviews. The particular national configuration of nursing and health care systems in each country is based on local health practices and organizational cultures — those deep-seated beliefs about the way work should be organized and the manner in which authority should be exercised. The American nurse who is consulting or working internationally must be knowledgeable about cultural differences concerning work, health, illness, health care, and health care delivery services. The time orientation of employees and both the short-range and strategic planning of management may vary considerably from American norms. The degree of expected individual initiative that is considered desirable for subordinates is most often significantly less in other countries than in the United States. Other potential differences include the individual and collective decision-making and control processes that the affect management mores and norms of the health care work force.

The major considerations for successful adaptation to a foreign organizational culture are recognition and acceptance of the definitions of nurse used in that country, and nursing's "place" in that organization. Factors involved include the career aspirations of the nurses, their social status, their occupational mobility, and their prior education. In some settings, political affiliation and sentiments within the country may have a major influence on management and practice.

Consulting in Other Countries

It is an exciting and humbling experience to receive invitations from countries around the world to share one's expertise as a consultant. When presented with the opportunity to visit another country as a consultant, there ensue particular professional and personal responsibilities. Of primary importance is expertise in the field you are being asked to address. For example, in health administration, the consultant should have substantial experience in the clinical practice of managing large work forces in health care systems, and have advanced academic preparation in health care administration. An ability to diagnose organizations and prepare the best possible briefing to assess designated areas of stated need, and to provide a variety of options and resources to meet those needs, are necessary requisites to the consultative process. The goal is for the client to be able to continue the process of change long after the consultant has returned to his or her home country.

Additionally, being a consultant is akin to being a guest in another person's home. Preparation for an international assignment should include studying the language and culture, even though a client country usually will provide translators. For example, in preparation for a lecture tour through Japan, I took a semester of conversational Japanese. In addition to basic social language skills, the class also provided practice in cultural body language and expected social conduct. During the trip, this background knowledge enabled a respectful communication process (with translator assistance). The classroom experience also assisted in gaining insight into the thoughts, ideas, and differences in the culture and health care practices of the host nation. A nurse consultant should always thoroughly research the health beliefs, health practices, and health care delivery systems of that country. While it may not always be possible to study the conversational language for a full semester, language and custom guides are readily available in most major bookstores, as well as travel guides and general information about almost any country.

The consultant also should request that the host country contact send in advance general information about the country's customs, monetary exchange, dress, culture, and religious practices. Such information may vitally affect the effectiveness of a consultant. For example, in Middle East countries such as Saudi Arabia, women are expected to dress covered from head to toe; short sleeves or short skirts are unacceptable, and may even result in arrest by religious police. Being a guest in another country means respecting that country's laws and customs concerning conduct, dress, etc.

Maintaining an entrepreneurial spirit and willingness to take action and risks, as well as having the courage to give direction to an organization unaccustomed to change, are necessary skills for assisting local nursing professionals to improve practice in ways not normally open to them. The most critical role of the consultant is to be an agent of feasible change, and then to work in conjunction with local managers to support and implement decisions.

Success in the consultant role requires a commitment to excellence in patient care while providing support to the client organization. Enthusiasm and an openness to ideas can generate excitement in any organizational setting. Through a consultant's endeavors at clarification, consistency, cooperation, integrity, and continuous growth, the nurturing of others becomes

the stimulation for the future of excellence in nursing and patient care (Brown 1986).

An Example of Assuming a Leadership Position in Another Country

This section will focus on my experiences as a nurse administrator in Saudi Arabia for over four years. This time frame included the Gulf War and presented the greatest administrative challenge ever experienced in my career.

Before going to Saudi Arabia, I studied the culture and language and talked with other women and nurses who had worked there. I also participated in a thorough orientation by the Hospital Corporation of America. I became aware that the presence of Mecca dominates Saudi life, and that the role of Saudi women has been in transition since the mid-1970s, when secondary schooling for women was introduced. Girls and boys are separated at puberty in all aspects of daily life. The traditional Saudi woman still lives a life primarily among only other women from her extended family, within the walls of her home compound. Women do not drive cars or work outside the home, and only venture outside with family members. My strong background in transcultural nursing was invaluable in understanding that my personal style of competence and assertiveness would have to be tempered for the successful performance of my job in Saudi Arabia.

Upon arrival, I was careful to follow local customs of dress, eating, and business. I practiced a lot of active listening skills and did not speak in meetings until called upon. As mutual respect developed, I began to be asked to participate more fully. I also concentrated on individually interviewing all medical chiefs of practice and all department heads about what they expected of nurses and nursing. Their responses lead to discussions about how I had seen nurses and nursing function elsewhere in other countries, and the strengths I had observed among the nurses practicing at the hospital.

This entry period allowed me to establish professional rapport with the major players on the management team. I also conducted an organizational assessment from observations, interviews, and review of past annual reports, financial summaries, and operations manuals. I then presented a brief, written report stating my assessment and the desired direction for the reorganization of nursing and patient care services, along with a recommendation for the hiring of additional advanced practice and administrative nurses to give direction to specialized practice. This document acted as a basic outline for the host country management team members to review, discuss, and respond to, and served as a springboard for them to later engage with me in developing a mutually agreed upon plan for growth and improvement of patient care.

The Saudi nursing staff members were truly international, and the hospital had developed different pay scales and job descriptions to reflect different levels of competence related to the type of basic nursing education each person had received. The majority of staff nurses had minimal and diverse nursing preparation, especially those from underdeveloped nations. Competency-based clinical standards were developed in order to objectively differentiate levels of practice and identify training needs. The goal was to elevate practice to current American standards. Certification programs and continuing education affiliated with the American Nurses Association provided nurses with both the challenge and motivation for self-development. When sufficient numbers of the nursing staff were able to perform the basic nursing process, including comprehensive patient assessment, confidence and competence were exemplified in improved patient care outcomes.

Nurses were now capable of communicating at a higher clinical level with physicians. Collaborative multidisciplinary practice committees were established, thereby improving problem-solving and decision-making processes and enhancing the working relationship between physicians, nurses, and other team members. This resulted in improved patient care. Seeing these positive changes among staff and in patient outcomes more than offset my personal cultural struggles in assuming this leadership position.

The challenges I faced were typical of those faced by many American or European nurses working as consultants to assist nurse administrators in other parts of the world to raise standards of nursing practice. Miriam Hirschfield (1992, p. 2) of the World Health Organization summarized such challenges in three statements: (1) "education, practice, and management must be developed jointly"; (2) "the need for nursing to take responsibility for caregiving wherever it may take place"; and (3) "nursing management has a major responsibility to develop the knowledge, skills, systems, and structures that will lead to the cost-effective provision of health care services."

Educating Nursing Administration Students in Other Countries

Advanced practice nursing administration is based on a synthesis of research and knowledge in nursing science, business administration, and other related disciplines. The Council on Graduate Education for Administration in Nursing recommends advanced education for nurses that includes content in: (1) nursing science and social science cognates; (2) nursing administration/management; (3) business administration/public administration/health care administration; and (4) methodology for program evaluation, research, accreditation, and grant writing. The program should include both didactic courses and practicum experiences, guided in the application of theories and skills introduced in didactic classes (Dienemann and Aroian 1994).

It is one thing to provide education in one's own country to foreign students so they can return to their country as leaders, but to attempt such education in a foreign setting, without the usual resources available to most graduate programs in nursing leadership and administration, is a far greater challenge.

Other considerations when accepting a position to teach administration of health care services in another country include the many cultural variables and social considerations that result in differences in faculty expectations and student learning styles. Different modes of thinking and expression are characteristic of foreign cultures. Students whose previous education differs radically from a U.S. educational environment will need instructors who can adapt their teaching styles to the social norms of that country.

Additionally, communicative competence, which involves sociolinguistic as well as grammatical competence, is an essential component in teaching leadership students in another country. Reliance on idiomatic expressions or Americanisms is inappropriate and interferes greatly with effective communication (Harrison 1992). Concrete examples appropriate to leadership roles in the host country, involving positive, neutral, and negative examples that may influence health care delivery, are key communication components. The curriculum must be flexibly adapted to the situation of the host country and its health care delivery system.

Conclusion

Common concerns for worldwide inequalities in health care goods and services and for social justice and the health of all people unite nurses all over the world to provide the strength and leadership necessary to create change that is so sorely needed. Such change includes actions to assist all people to be able to meet their basic health needs, beginning with access to the means for maintaining healthy and hygienic living conditions and the opportunity to receive nursing care for at least the most common health deviations.

American nurses might well be reminded of the historical development of the nursing profession in the United States when considering international consultation. It was British nurses who brought the Nightingale model for nursing education and practice to our shores in the mid-1850s. Since then, American nursing has faced and overcome severe nurse shortages; a dearth in leaders well-prepared in practice, education, and research; and continuing political challenges reflecting low status as a profession. However, as one reflects on the evolution of nursing and the constant conflict and discourse regarding professional status and the requirement of a baccalaureate degree for entry into practice, the gap between the evolution of nursing in the United States and international settings narrows (Brown 1990).

Summary of Issues

1. Americans are recruited to consult and/or teach in other countries without necessarily having the requisite experience and/or academic knowledge to be effective.

2. Americans' lack of bilingual and transcultural knowledge impedes their effectiveness as consultants.

3. Competency-based nursing practice utilizes the nursing process as an effective way for improving patient outcomes worldwide.

4. Standards exist to identify the essentials for nursing administration education

worldwide. Concrete local examples for cultural adaptation and application need to be added when developing a curriculum for another country.

5. There is a need to develop nursing clinical practice, administration, and education in other countries in order to improve caregiving worldwide.

Recommended Strategies

1. Make an organizational assessment and diagnosis before making recommendations for change.

2. Nurses should only accept consulting offers for which they have sufficient clinical, educational, and consultative experience to execute competently.

3. When accepting international assignments, nurses should obtain cultural awareness and language training specific to the host country before departure.

4. The World Health Organization (WHO) and the International Council of Nurses (ICN) should cooperatively support the global development of post-secondary educational programs for nurses in clinical practice, management, and education.

5. Professional nursing associations should offer training programs in international health and consulting for nursing leaders.

6. American schools of nursing should create faculty and student exchange opportunities with other countries in order to increase cultural competence and an awareness of other health care delivery systems.

Preferred Outcomes

1. Collaborative international consultation will provide leverage for the worldwide implementation of competency-based nursing practice.

2. American nursing consultants will act in a culturally appropriate manner.

3. Flexible adaptation of curricula and teaching methods by Americans and others teaching in international settings will provide culturally appropriate excellence in education.

4. American nurses with appropriate education and experience will effectively assume nursing leadership positions in other countries.

References

Brown, B.J. 1986. From the editor. Nursing Administration Quarterly 10 (4): iv-v.

_____. 1990. A world view of nursing practice: An international perspective. In The nursing profession: Turning points, ed. N. Chaska, pp. 406-414. St. Louis: C.V. Mosby.

Dienemann, J. and Aroian, J., eds. 1994. Essentials of baccalaureate level nursing education for nursing leadership and management and essentials of master's level nursing education for nursing administration advanced practice. Unpublished report for the Council on Graduate Education in Nursing, Chapel Hill, N.C.

Harrison, M. 1992. Toward effective intercultural teaching. On the scene: King Faisal Specialist Hospital and Research Centre, Riyadh, Saudi Arabia. Nursing Administration Quarterly 16 (2): 29-24.

Hirschfield, M. 1992. Challenges from the World Health Organization. Nursing Administration Quarterly 16 (2): 2.

[0] This chapter is based on the author's experiences as a consultant, educator, and practicing administrator in Israel, England, China, Japan, Singapore, New Zealand, Taiwan, Italy, Saudi Arabia, Jordan, Egypt, Greece, and Guam.

Chapter 7
Culturally Competent Care: What Is an Administrator To Do?

Claudette G. Varricchio, DSN, RN, OCN, FAAN

The United States is rapidly shifting toward a more racially, ethnically diverse population. Based on U.S. Census Bureau reports, it is estimated that by 2050, the majority of people living in this country will belong to groups now called "minorities" (Voelker 1995). This shift, reflected in the makeup of both patient and nursing populations, mandates a more culturally competent work force to deliver appropriate health care in our changing society.

The American Nurses Association's Council on Cultural Diversity in Nursing Practice, in a 1991 position statement, recommended that:

Nurse administrators need to foster policies and procedures that help ensure access to care that accommodates varying cultural beliefs. Nurse administrators need to be knowledgeable about, and sensitive to, the diversity among providers and consumers.

In order to do this, nurse administrators must foster a climate in which nurses and other health care providers understand that provider-patient "encounters include the interaction of three cultural systems: the culture of the health care provider, the culture of the client, and the culture of the setting" (American Nurses Association 1991).

Nurse administrators in practice and education are responsible for setting expectations and goals, thus providing the resources and climate in which culturally competent care is established as an institu-

tional value. The goal is to provide optimal care for all people. This cannot be done unless the cultural and ethnic influences on an individual's concept of health and illness, including the accepted cultural responses to symptoms and other distressing events, are understood and incorporated into the practice of health care professionals. A nurse administrator has the responsibility to create a structure that supports a climate in which cultural competence can flourish. The administrator also needs to actively reinforce the critical importance of culture in the delivery of effective health care.

Creating a Vision

A steering committee should be chosen, made up of administrators and clinicians representing the major health professions providing care in the institution, with an ethnic mix representative of the patient population served. The committee's mission will be to identify the current cultural appropriateness of care delivered, create a vision of what it should be, and then devise strategies to transform the system in order to provide culturally appropriate care.

For behavior to be cultural, it must be learned and shared by the members of a given group (Galanti 1991). For care to be appropriate, it must be assessed as acceptable to the patient. Such an assessment requires knowledge not only of different cultures, but also of the specific culture a patient belongs to, and the degree to which he or she is acculturated to Western medicine and the health care standards of the organization.

Once a vision is stated, the steering committee's next task will be to adopt a framework to use in referring to culturally appropriate care for patients from various cultures. The goals are to understand how different cultures define a psychologically healthy individual, to reinforce the family's acculturation function, and to define the concept of community in terms of size and who is included (Locke 1992). A common first step is examining literature on transcultural nursing, medical anthropology, critical theory in sociology, and cross-cultural education. Campinha-Bacote (1991) suggests searching all readings for concrete direction to guide nursing practice. Specific information is needed on how to address the cultural phenomena evident in all cultural groups, and how the global interactions of cultural groups are expressed in the values, beliefs, and actions of a specific individual. A helpful framework should include variations in communication, social and personal space, the social organization of hierarchies within the culture, time and temporal orientation, environmental control, and biology (Rajan 1995). An alternative approach to understanding minority cultures in relation to a dominant culture involves an assessment of the cultural group's degree of acculturation, history of poverty and oppression, language and arts, racism and prejudice, sociopolitical factors, child-rearing practices, religious practices, family structure, and values and attitudes (Locke 1992).

Humanism is often proposed as nursing's guiding principle in providing holistic, culturally appropriate care to individuals, families, and communities. This concept is insufficiently concrete to guide the delivery of care and hold nurses accountable for culturally competent care. As Mulholland (1995, p. 433) states, "A central component of humanist approaches within nursing has been a failure to contextualize the interaction between the individual and his or her social context in any rigorous manner."

A framework should be chosen that all members of the organization recognize as sufficient to guide clinicians in gaining knowledge and understanding of the dominant culture and other cultures represented among staff, patients, families, and the local community. This framework should be used to guide training, standards of care and practice, policies, strategic initiatives, and evaluations.

Providing Training

To create a climate in which culturally sensitive care can flourish, the administrator provides assistance by requiring staff participation in cultural sensitivity training that explores culture, ethnicity, race, acculturation, patient expectations, and caregiver attitudes. A favorable climate is created when this training is presented during the working day, rather than during personal time or as a part of formal curriculum offerings. This time investment emphasizes the value put on cultural competence by the organization (Shanahan and Brayshaw 1995).

Cultural sensitivity training begins with increasing staff members' awareness of their own cultural beliefs and personal diversity. Paniagua (1994) suggests using the Brief Acculturation Scale for self-assessment. The subscales for self-evaluation of biases and prejudice can be useful in increasing caregivers' sensitivity to the concept of cultural difference that is needed before changes in practice that lead to culturally sensitive care can be instituted. Another component of cultural sensitivity training involves clarification of terms such as culture, ethnicity, race, and acculturation.

People differ not only as to the cultures and ethnic groups with which they identify, but also as to the degree they identify with the dominant ethnic group (Wilkinson 1993). Acculturation is the degree to which members of a given ethnic group have immersed themselves in the culture of the dominant group. According to Locke (1992, p. 6), degrees of acculturation may be described as:

1. Bicultural: able to function as effectively in the dominant culture as in one's own, while still holding on to manifestations of the culture of origin.

2. Traditional: holding on to a majority of cultural traits from the culture of origin, while rejecting many of the traits of the dominant culture.

3. Marginal: having little real contact with traits of either culture.

4. Acculturated: having given up most of the cultural traits of the culture of origin and assumed the traits of the dominant culture.

In defining the degree of acculturation, it should be recognized that the differences within a cultural group may be greater than the differences between it and the dominant culture.

The next step in training is an active involvement in building skills for the valuing and managing of diversity. Otherwise, the new knowledge about other cultures could be used merely as a checklist for any patient who seems to be of a particular origin; in other words, training might reinforce stereotypical behavior instead of reducing it. This step includes education in cultural assessment, culture brokering, and conflict management. The nursing staff needs to be trained to effectively use the cultural assessment tool chosen by the steering committee. Education must go beyond assessment to the adaptation of care, with an emphasis on the uniqueness of each person. Staff members might otherwise see cultural assessment as just one more form to be completed. The goal of individualizing care according to the unique acculturation and ethnic identity of each patient must be emphasized and reinforced in the practice setting.

Nurses should be reassured that they are not expected to fully understand the cultural beliefs and behaviors of everyone they may encounter in practice. Instead, training should include how to use cultural intermediaries as culture brokers (Fuller 1995). These cultural intermediaries may be professional or paraprofessional health care workers who come from the same culture as the patient, or a more acculturated family member or interpreter who can help to bridge the cultural gap and explain some of the meanings of culturally specific perceptions to the nurse and to the patient. These interactions will assist nurses in communicating with patients without using jargon, and will increase their ability to step outside of the ethnocentric "professional model" of traditional Western medicine (Anderson 1990).

Adopting a Standardized Cultural Assessment

Assessment of the patient's perspective can be guided by the use of acculturation scales originally designed as research instruments, such as the Brief Acculturation Scale mentioned earlier. There are many available scales that have been normed and validated on specific cultural groups; however, all are not suited for clinical use. Other sources of cultural assessment tools include transcultural nursing texts and practice journals, although these usually lack rigorous testing. Anderson (1990, p. 138), building on the work of Kleinman, Eisenberg, and Good (1978), summarized ways to assess the patient's perspective as eight questions that could be used to bridge the gap between understanding and interpreting cultural influences on health, compliance, and other treatment concepts.

1. What do you think has caused your problem?

2. Why do you think it started when it did?

3. What do you think your sickness does to you? How does it work?

4. How severe is your sickness? Will it have a short or a long course?

5. What kind of treatment do you think you should receive?

6. What are the most important results you hope to receive from this treatment?

7. What are the chief problems your sickness has caused for you?

8. What do you fear most about your sickness?

Group consensus should agree that any chosen assessment tool fits within the framework used by the organization and is seen as useful by all the health disciplines. After the steering committee makes its selection, a policy and procedure should be developed and reviewed by all bodies governing patient care before being adopted. A tool that nurses, physicians, or social workers reject as not feasible for use in practice will not be used to improve patient care.

Institutionalizing Cultural Competence

The system that has as its goal culturally competent care must set standards for cultural assessment, diagnosis, intervention, and evaluation. Cultural concepts such as acculturation should be incorporated into the standard assessment and history format used by the institution. The institutional expectations stated in standards of care and professional practice must be revised in order to ensure that the patient's perspective on health, illness, causation, and health practices is identified and appropriately applied in providing care. Cultural assessment also must be reflected in a defined place in the patient record, policy and procedure manuals, orientation and training programs, quality improvement programs, and patient outcome measures. Adaptation of care for cultural appropriateness should be incorporated into critical pathways and case management plans during the management of care and tracking of patient outcomes. This will facilitate program evaluation of culturally specific interventions. The provision of culturally appropriate care also should be a line item in all performance evaluation criteria and forms. Nurses must be rewarded for meeting the challenge of providing quality care to persons of differing cultural groups (Galanti 1991).

The institution's strategic plan should include specific objectives regarding the cultural competence of staff and care delivery. A timetable and responsibility chart need to be developed to ensure accountability and continued institutional commitment to this substantial change in practice. These changes will require time for creation, acceptance, and assimilation by staff. This array of structural changes will support training and other initiatives to incorporate culturally competent care as a norm within the institution.

Conclusion

The goals of culturally competent care are to improve patient compliance with the therapeutic plan, foster greater respect for diversity, increase understanding of specific cultures through knowledge, decrease racism and ethnocentrism, and promote more satisfactory interactions between nurse and client (Campinha-Bacote 1991). These goals will lead to better care of the patient whose cultural environment differs from that of the nurse. They also may lead to better compliance with therapeutic goals and, therefore, shortened stays or decreased complications. An indirect advantage may be that the institution will be recognized as sympathetic to culturally diverse clients and become the place of choice to seek health care.

Disadvantages to implementing culturally competent care include the fact that, initially, the teaching, learning, and institutionalization of such care will consume additional resources of personnel time and energy. There will be costs for implementation that may include translators, interpreters, or other intermediaries for communication with patients who speak another language, or who have a minimal command of English. There is the constant risk of incorrectly labeling the patient and ignoring individual differences within cultures, or making false assumptions about the degree of acculturation of the individual (Campinha-Bacote 1991). However, the advantages far outweigh the costs and risks involved. The new demographic face of our communities and our country creates an imperative for initiating and sustaining efforts to enhance cultural awareness, in order to effectively provide quality, culturally competent nursing care.

Summary of Issues

1. Cultural diversity among Americans is rapidly increasing.

2. Most health care institutions employ a professional model of ethnocentric Western medicine in the delivery of health care.

3. Nurse administrators in both practice and educational settings are responsible for the degree to which staff members function in a culturally competent manner.

Recommended Strategies

1. A steering committee will be formed to strategically plan for the institutionalization of cultural competence in schools of nursing and health services facilities.

2. Institutions will concurrently train employees and revise policies and procedures to support culturally competent practice.

3. An evaluation of the effects of cultural competence will be incorporated into quality improvement, program evaluation, critical paths, and case management in health care facilities.

4. An evaluation of the effects of cultural competence will be incorporated into grading criteria, program evaluation, faculty promotion and tenure guidelines, and accreditation in schools of nursing.

Preferred Outcomes

1. Nurse administrators will adopt the American Nurses Association's 1991 position statement on cultural diversity in nursing practice.

2. Cultural competence will become institutionalized in both schools of nursing and health services facilities.

3. Administrators will conclude that the benefits of culturally competent care outweigh the costs.

References

American Nurses Association, Council on Cultural Diversity in Nursing Practice. 1991. Cultural diversity in nursing practice. Position statement, Kansas City, Mo.

Anderson, J.M. 1990. Health across cultures. Nursing Outlook 38 (3): 136-139.

Campinha-Bacote, J. 1991. The process of cultural competence. Wyoming, Ohio: Transcultural C.A.R.E. Associates.

Fuller, J. 1995. Challenging old notions of professionalism: How can nurses work with paraprofessional ethnic health workers? Journal of Advanced Nursing 22: 465-472.

Galanti, G.A. 1991. Caring for patients from different cultures. Philadelphia: University of Pennsylvania Press.

Kleinman, A.; Eisenberg, L.; and Good, B. 1978. Culture, illness, and care: Clinical lessons from anthropologic and cross-cultural research. Annals of Internal Medicine 88: 351-358.

Locke, D.C. 1992. Increasing multicultural understanding. Newbury Park, Calif.: Sage.

Mulholland, J. 1995. Nursing, humanism, and transcultural theory: The "bracketing out of reality." Journal of Advanced Nursing 22: 442-449.

Paniagua, F.A. 1994. Assessing and treating culturally diverse clients. Thousand Oaks, Calif.: Sage.

Rajan, M.F.J. 1995. Transcultural nursing: A perspective derived from Jean-Paul Sarte. Journal of Advanced Nursing 22: 450-455.

Shanahan, M. and Brayshaw, D.L. 1995. Are nurses aware of the differing health care needs of Vietnamese patients? Journal of Advanced Nursing 22: 456-464.

Voelker, R. 1995. Speaking the languages of medicine and culture. Journal of the American Medical Association 273 (21): 1629-1641.

Wilkinson, D. 1993. Family ethnicity in America. In Family ethnicity: Strength in diversity, ed. H.P McAdoo, pp. 15-59. Newbury Park, Calif.: Sage.

Chapter 8
Cocreation of Culture through Choice

JoEllen Goertz Koerner, PhD, RN, FAAN

As the world becomes increasingly multi-dimensional and multicultural, the need for a worldview and value system that brings this richness of diversity into some coherent pattern of unity is essential. We are bombarded daily with multiple examples of fragmentation and alienation from ourselves, from each other, and from the natural environment in which we dwell. The call for holism, which confronts society as we become a transglobal village, is foundational to nursing practice; it is embedded into our social contract with society. Thus, as nurse administrators take the lead in designing and implementing clinical care systems, a recognition and expression of diversity must be creatively woven into a rich culture of coherence and healing.

Coherent Worldviews in a Changing Society

Each of us comprises a running total of every moment we ever have experienced and all information we ever have acquired. At the personal level, our worldview is a theme running through our life — a thread that weaves together disparate pieces into a coherent whole. To acquire this sense of order, we seek patterns of decision making that carry us toward increasing order and unity with our values. If we fail to find and use patterns consistent with our worldview, we don't know who we are; we are alienated from ourselves.

At the social level, our worldview links the many elements of our myriad relationships with other people, groups, and cul-

tures. We adopt things such as language, symbols, shared aspirations, and interests because they express who we are. A feeling of belonging and moral agency flows from unity among relationships. If we fail to develop a coherent worldview at the social level, our sense of belonging breaks down, leaving us feeling alienated from society.

Finally, at the spiritual level, our worldview is a theme that integrates a sense of self, of belonging, of the sacred, and of a relatedness between us and the wider world — nature, the environment, the planet, the universe. Philosophical questions about the meaning of life, the purpose of our existence, the role of suffering, and our desire to do good are pondered in this domain. Without a coherent worldview, our sense of self and our place in the world disintegrates; we feel dispirited and empty.

A successful worldview draws all these levels — personal, social, and spiritual — into a coherent whole, giving individuals a sense of who they are, why they are here, and how they relate to others. Zohar (1990) observes that we become aware of our worldview only when our present one is inadequate or changing. Today's rapidly changing environment is reducing coherence in people's lives and forcing them to adopt new worldviews. The success or failure in reestablishing coherence ultimately rests with individuals' awareness of their own experiences, their deepest intuitions, and their knowledge of the world and themselves in it. As Carl Jung (Hollingsworth 1964, p. 149) observed, "In the last analysis, the essential thing is the life of the individual.... We make our own epoch."

Culture as a Lived Choice

Culture is the foundation for coherence in the world. It is a complex and multidimensional phenomenon. We each have unique and personal values that are solely our own, and simultaneously share many values with the world around us. Culture is both internal (the essence of our personal value system) and external (the social context in which we live). As poet John Donne observed, "No man is an island, entire of itself; every man is a piece of the continent, a part of the main" (Bartlett's 16th ed.). To be involved with oneself is to simultaneously be involved with others, though often we are only partially aware of it. A shared culture, one that aligns certain aspects of who we are and how we express ourselves, also acknowledges the ethical nature of connectedness. The developmental thrust in our lives is toward moral maturity.

The act of living requires a series of daily choices, both large and small. We must decide, for instance, what to eat, where to go, and how to be with others. Choice patterns reflect our worldview and are expressed as values shaping the direction and events of our life. As human beings, we are composed of both genetically determined bodies and minds that reflect the experiences we have lived. These inseparable qualities create the meeting point between what we are and what we are becoming. At this juncture, daily decisions are made through an ongoing dialogue with our past, our current existence, the environment, and other experiences. Through this dialogue, our values influence the various choices we make. They determine how the choice fits into the total context of our lives (Zohar 1990). Though worldview alone does not determine the choices we make, it does play a crucial role in making some choices more likely than others; each choice influences the next. Over time, the probability of making a particular choice increases, giving pattern and constancy to our lives. The entire history and makeup of our being increases the probability of certain choice patterns. In time, choice patterns tend to become ingrained into habit;

we make them with little thought or expenditure of energy. This leaves our conscious mind free to process other issues and information in creative new ways. However, we are always free to choose against the weight of probability and the bondage of habit. It is this freedom to choose that makes us creative, responsible, and adaptable humans.

To deny people the freedom to make choices consistent with their worldviews is to do them violence (Chittister 1990). Therefore, in an era of increasing contact between diverse peoples and ideas, nurse administrators need to cocreate environments filled with choices and options in order to foster a culture of pluralistic comfort, synergy, and creativity.

We have a moral imperative to use our freedom of choice to be in touch with the fearsome edge of our consciousness, constantly reshaping our worldview to maintain coherence in a changing world. Gilmore, Hirschhorn, and O'Connor (1994) observe that the long-term solution to the management of change involves helping individuals develop a greater maturity in understanding and managing the boundaries between their own inner worlds and the realities of the external environment. With maturity, people meet new challenges, make new relationships, chart new paths, and grow. Creation of order out of chaos does not refer to "tidying up," but rather to creating a new order and set of relationships that give rise to coherent, relational wholes — utterly transforming both old meanings and previous potential (Wheatley 1992). The capacity to spontaneously create order from chaos is the basis of creativity in all living systems.

Cocreating a Shared Culture

The complexity of existence finds us enmeshed in several cultures simultaneously. We carry a genetic DNA and a culture from our family of origin. Simultaneously, we become members of the social group formed by the geography in which we reside. We also are members of a culture in our workplaces, where we often spend as many waking hours as in our homes. Learning the culturally determined codes of behavior for these various settings requires time and energy. The learning process is easier, however, if our worldview is particularly aligned with the predominant cultural mores of a specific setting and with the relationships that support them.

Our country is rapidly increasing in cultural diversity, which is reflected in the increasingly varied cultural makeup of employees in health care organizations. This change presents an opportunity for health care organizations to replace old values of homogeneity with new ones that value diversity. It is the diversity of human skills and unpredictability of the human spirit that make initiative, creativity, and entrepreneurship possible. Our health care organizations can become shared entrepreneurial enterprises if we are willing to transform our culture. In such organizations, the commitment, creativity, and entrepreneurship of employees, rather than fiscal and material assets, become the essential capital for success (Bartlett and Ghoshal 1994).

Capitalizing on diversity requires giving up a monolithic culture that minimizes individuality. Old structures that reinforce the monolithic culture must be discarded in order to create new wholes that facilitate unique, as well as collective, ways of being (Bartlett and Ghoshal 1995a). Old behaviors by managers, clinicians, and support staff also must change. Everyone in the organization must be committed to fulfilling the social contract the health care system has with the people it serves. Mutual commitment is built through shared worldviews and goals. All employees, clinicians, and managers need a vision of corporate ambition, passion, and purpose. This vision is then translated into visible and measurable goals that employees can internalize and emulate.

Organizational goals are reinforced by adjusting personnel, recruitment, development, and assignment policies. Reward systems also need to change to reflect the lived experiences of the entire organization. For instance, recognizing that star employees can only succeed because a critical mass is carrying out the foundational work on which their success is built leads to celebrating the individual contributions and accomplishments of all employees, rather than those of only the superstars. A culture that celebrates the extraordinary value of the ordinary done well is truly honoring the uniqueness of each individual.

The health care organization must commit to developing employees' capacity for personal growth, in addition to their task competencies. The organization must foster individual initiative, accountability, and style by openly sharing information and decision-making processes (Bartlett and Ghoshal 1995b). Clinicians and support staff must give up conformity and security for a new beginning in which they use initiative to seize opportunities to expand their organizational value and to actively participate in resolving organizational dilemmas.

Managers must learn to ask new questions about employees, such as, "What special environment or what metaphor for growth will help this person thrive?" That is what we must focus on as we bring individuals into the new work groups of the health care organization. As Rabbi Machman said, "God calls one person with a song, one with a shout, one with a whisper" (LeShan 1995, p. 65). It is this kind of individuating focus that must permeate the purposes and processes of emerging systems. In these organizations, management's purpose is not to make decisions and control others in order to make them conform; it is to facilitate employees' entrepreneurial decision making and creative expression of themselves in order to provide culturally and technically competent health care.

Increased diversity and access to information also will create healthy conflicts and challenges to old underlying assumptions about work. Such a dramatic change in expectations often will produce uncertainty and confusion. Training and reinforcement of problem-solving and conflict management skills must accompany the downward movement of decision making in order to reduce defensiveness and prevent costly chaos. The introduction of continuous quality improvement and shared governance systems is one example of giving democratic decision-making and evaluation processes to frontline employees. Through interactions that are face-to-face, cross-functional, and cross-divisional in nature, staff members begin to see the interrelatedness of their work. Such a broad systems perspective replaces the narrow sense of "us versus them," which has proven so divisive in the past.

To actualize this new organizational form, management's key role is to cocreate a culture for initiative. Managers must truly hold individual employee capability in high esteem. The goal is a reliance on peer evaluation and self-discipline, in order for each person to seek and gain skills to sustain personal competence. The purpose of management thus changes from controlling others' behavior to providing mutually agreed upon performance standards and the necessary resources to achieve them. A sense of mutual interdependence and community is fostered. Employee dependence on formal control systems is minimized as managers coach individuals in self-monitoring and self-correcting behaviors in real-time situations, instead of intervening with corrective actions.

Another important aspect of cocreating a new culture is for the organization to foster the letting go of "old ways." Key management personnel must be deployed throughout the organization to facilitate strategic thinking at all levels. One method of facilitation is face-to-face dialogue about problems and their past, future, and contextual interpretations, providing both the manager and others with a teaching-learning exchange. In this way, the information becomes richer, revealing peaks and troughs, as well as averages. Rich information is the lifeblood for creative growth, for individuals as well as for the organization. We must look at data in new ways — seeing new relationships, and noting the subtle as well as the obvious. Another parallel activity to facilitate strategic thinking is to identify opportunities for "unlearning experiences" — helping individuals to recognize their own limiting assumptions and to break old habits that no longer are productive.

Sustaining a Life-Giving Culture

Our adherence to an organizational culture flows from a commitment to participate, which is renewed time and time again. When there is similarity between individual and organizational values, individuals become more committed and more productive. They become more entangled with others through choice and repetition. Each day the commitment is renewed in various large and small ways; the shared experiences create memories that are woven deeply into our beings. Identities overlap and personal qualities become more aligned, more correlated. Both the relationships and the individuals grow accordingly.

Active work is required to develop, sustain, and deepen relationships within a group or culture. This may take the subtle form of adherence to or renewal of certain values cherished by the group or culture, or through the observance of rituals and ceremonies. For example, the celebration of anniversaries and public holidays, the joint singing of national anthems and football cheers, and the shared reverence for symbols such as flags all lay down patterns in our consciousness that bring us more deeply into correlation with others in our culture. To the extent that we participate, we feel, on the social level of existence, more or less at home, more or less alienated, more or less empty. Relationships are sustained and deepened through the observance of rituals that create powerful memories.

Ritual organizes the past, encoding it in symbol form. In observing ritual, we draw the past and all of our observations of it into the present and integrate it with our current experience. Organizations and professions encode values in ritual and symbol to elevate their presence and importance as ways of being in the world. An example of organizational ritual is the graduation ceremonies that end an academic year, with each professor donning hood and gown as new graduates are welcomed into professional life. Health care organizations often celebrate Nurse's Day with a ceremony in which members of management honor nurses to show appreciation for their contributions.

In its evolution, nursing has discarded the cap, a symbol long associated with the profession; the ritual of capping and pinning in schools of nursing is no longer a rite of passage into full professional status. Currently, the profession is woefully lacking an adequate replacement ritual that draws past and future into a powerful present. This lack of ritual reflects nursing's current identity struggle as the health care industry evolves. We must carefully examine nursing's essence and encode it in new symbols, or reinterpret the old in relevant ways, if we are to stay grounded in our origins and our purpose to society.

Conclusion

For executives, leading and synergizing a new worldview for the health care organization requires a great deal. LeShan (1995) identifies two levels of role modeling required of leaders. First-level modeling occurs in the daily interaction with others, living in such a way that you pay attention to your sense of self, respecting yourself. What one is attempting to teach here is an attitude, but it cannot be taught; it can only be "caught" as one is exposed to it. Moreover, this message is reinforced or negated by second-level role modeling, which is revealed through the leader's self-development: does he/she take as much time and energy caring for his/her own growth and "becoming" as he/she does for his/her subordinates? Another way to state this is, if in any five-year period he/she isn't having a better time and more fun in life than in a previous five-year period, he/she should be barred from leadership.

LeShan (1995) further observes that we have a beautiful, joyous, wonderful, crazy, sick, neurotic, pathological culture. Nurses, too, are all of these things, and have so much potential. The question is, can we learn to be with ourselves and with others in new ways? We are in a period of transition — in an age that is dying as a new one is being born. Humanity's history demonstrates that life's force is always geared toward greater wholeness and integration. As we develop the skill of pluralistic comfort, we will be well-prepared to honor the uniqueness of the individual and to facilitate the integration of the collective in order to more effectively heal humanity and ourselves.

Summary of Issues

1. The rapidly changing environment is creating situations that cause people to question their worldviews.

2. A culture of pluralistic comfort, synergy, and democracy is a possible choice for health services agencies and educational organizations.

3. A culture that values and manages diversity must be cocreated by all members of an organization in order to be realized.

4. Managers need to acknowledge the creativity and entrepreneurship existing at all levels of the organization.

5. The rituals and symbols of nursing either have lost their meaning or have been abandoned.

Recommended Strategies

1. Invest time and energy in building a shared vision and shared governance as the foundation for work among health care personnel, patients, families, communities, faculty, and students.

2. Assess the symbolic meaning of the myths, heroes, rituals, and ceremonies present in the organization and realign them to support the desired new culture.

3. Replace formal work flow systems with people-centered processes that allow for flexible creativity in achieving work goals.

4. Provide timely, meaningful information to each group and employee concerning the quality, history, context, and value of their work.

5. Develop new rituals, ceremonies, and symbols for nursing and the organization of nursing services that celebrate individuals and reinforce nursing's contract with society.

Preferred Outcomes

1. Top management will choose to cocreate new organizational cultures that value uniqueness and fully engage each employee and student.

2. Clinicians, managers, support staff, faculty, and students will share a culture that fosters compatible worldviews of work, health, illness, and nursing.

3. Health services agencies and schools of nursing will foster individual initiative and style.

4. Increased group and individual self-discipline, accountability for productivity, personal growth, and expanding competence will emerge.

5. Nursing will have a clear identity, shared by nurses, their colleagues, and society.

References

Bartlett, C.A. and Ghoshal, S. 1994. Changing the role of top management: Beyond strategy to purpose. Harvard Business Review 72 (6): 79-88.

. 1995a. Changing the role of top management: Beyond structure to processes. Harvard Business Review 73 (1): 86-96.

. 1995b. Changing the role of top management: Beyond systems to people. Harvard Business Review 73 (2): 132-142.

Bartlett's Familiar Quotations, 16th ed., s.v. "island, no man is an," 231:8.

Chittister, J. 1990. Wisdom distilled from the daily. San Francisco: Harper.

Gilmore, T.; Hirschhorn, L.; and O'Connor, M. 1994. The boundaryless organization. Healthcare Forum Journal 7 (4): 68-72.

Hollingsworth, D., ed. 1964. C.G. Jung: The collected works, vol. 10. London: Routledge & Kegan Paul.

LeShan, L. 1995. Mobilizing the life force, treating the individual. Alternative Therapies 1(1): 63-69.

Wheatley, M. 1992. Leadership and the new science. San Francisco: Barrett-Koehler.

Zohar, D. 1990. The quantum self: Human nature and consciousness defined by the new physics. New York: Quill/William Morrow.

Chapter 9
Transforming Health Care through Cultural Competence Training

Noel J. Chrisman, PhD, MPH
Phyllis R. Schultz, PhD, RN, FAAN

Respect is an attitude toward others that is grounded, theoretically, in an acceptance of shared participation in a common moral community, or, at least, of a common humanity. The need for respect to be nurtured (in education) and required (in practice) typically arises from students' and practitioners' challenging encounters with difference; e.g., of beliefs, rituals, speech, symbols, power status, gender, ethnicity, or sexual orientation. A respectful attitude values the core of humanity in the "other" without necessarily admiring or even approving of the beliefs or other differences as noted. Actions arising from respect are sometimes known as basic courtesies (Lenburg et al. 1995, p. 37).

In an era of rapid restructuring of the health care system and significant demographic and political shifts in the American landscape (Shugars, O'Neil, and Bader 1991; O'Neil 1993), there is a clear-cut need for health care organizations to open themselves to the social, cultural, economic, and political diversity of their communities. To accomplish this change, which has become a matter of survival as well as of service, the institutions themselves will need to undergo a transformation to enhance respect for diversity and to expand the skills to actualize that respect in health care services.

We believe that the changes we are all experiencing will underpin a paradigm shift in the ways we think about health care. The position of the traditionally privileged white middle class has often been to reject others on grounds of race, social class, gender, sexual orientation, disability, etc. Reciprocal hostilities among those rejected have developed and festered. Similarly, many health care providers have avoided serious consideration of the strengths of cultural solutions to illness, such as folk remedies or folk healers. Practitioners have not attended to the extent to which American citizens of all cultures use family and alternative medical resources (Eisenberg et al. 1993; Zola 1972). Thus, disruptions in the fabric of the health care system diminish efforts and outcomes among staff, erode patient care, and increase discord.

What is occurring now is a change from viewing cultural diversity as an impediment to the "real and legitimate" work of health care to viewing diversity as strengthening the work force by enhancing creativity and generating stronger ties with the community. In addition, health professionals are beginning to see that cultural competence in clinical care improves practitioner-patient relationships. To support this trend, we need to provide training programs that help people move beyond statements that they already recognize individual uniqueness, that they do not stereotype others, and that they are not racist — helping them build relationships rather than blame others for a system that does not work. Similarly, training programs need to expand the existing skills of clinicians in order to assess and work with the increasing variety of family responses to illness. If the health care system is to survive in the context of a global economy and increasing demographic change, the goals that we must aim for are simple to articulate and yet difficult to achieve: multiculturalism and the celebration of diversity.

This chapter's review of training for culturally competent care reveals some commonalties that can be scrutinized for their actual or likely contributions to the realization of these goals. We will describe currently available training, delineate its strengths and limitations, identify the preferred outcomes, and offer recommendations for how to move beyond the current situation to where we want to be.

Examples of Programs

An examination of the kinds of competency training available to health care institutions reveals a wide variety of conferences, training modules, classes, and in-service workshops that have been used by hospitals and other health care organizations. Frequently, however, activities have been carried out piecemeal, leading to incomplete coverage of staff and only a surface understanding of culture and diversity. For example, a number of institutions have provided diversity workshops to managers on the assumption that they will teach these skills to their teams. Although evidence is only anecdotal, the managers in most cases are neither properly trained nor adequately motivated to accomplish such a lofty goal. The inventory that follows constitutes a set of resources that can and should be used by leaders in health care organizations. Readers should be aware of the fact that any of these workshops may be presented alone, but that for the paradigm shift to occur, changes in mission, structure, training, and individual commitment also must occur.

Generic Programs

The two most frequent types of training can be called valuing diversity and managing diversity. Valuing diversity is a basic element in cultural competence that is primarily focused on learning about oneself in relation to others who are different in a variety of ways. Here is where discussions and exercises referring to the broader sense of diversity (e.g., race, class, gender, etc.) are most readily found. In many cases, these workshops focus explicitly on power relations within the institution, a difficult but essential topic. Workshops on valuing diversity tend to be highly interactive, both between the trainer and participants and among participants. Frequently, hospitals/ agencies will hire companies that provide diversity training; in some cases, a trainer has been invited to simply give a lecture about racism or other forms of interpersonal harm. Thus, the message is generic and can be aimed at all personnel in a health care organization. When clinicians direct these workshops, there is a higher likelihood that examples will be drawn from experiences shared among health provider participants. This is not essential, however, for it is all aspects of daily life experiences that form the foundation of these workshops. A benefit to providing workshops on valuing diversity for all personnel — providers and support staff — is that the message is conveyed that this is an institutional goal and activity, and that all employees are in this together.

The basic goal of valuing diversity workshops is teaching people to prevent insult to each other (Kavanagh and Kennedy 1992) and to promote good cross-cultural communication skills (e.g., Pederson 1988). A typical set of topics might include:

- Learning about Differences

- The Dynamics of Difference (a particularly useful concept outlined by Cross et al. 1989)

- Identifying Personal Experiences

- Increasing Self-Knowledge

- "Prevention of Insult" Skills

- Multicultural Communications

Achievement of these objectives typically takes six to eight hours or more.

Busy clinicians much prefer the one-shot, one-hour lecture that leaves their biomedical paradigm intact, and their personal opinions unaltered. An institutional approach that requires universal attendance might circumvent this problem by exposing all personnel to the same conditions. In addition, one of the most significant barriers to valuing and celebrating diversity will be reduced in strength: the belief that one group (frequently physicians) is privileged and is not required to change behavior. An equally common problem that constantly must be monitored is the existence of new employees or employees who miss the workshop. Like the privileged group, nonattendees neither learn the new information nor share the sense of a common goal that is part of well-designed diversity workshops. These individuals are less likely to change their behavior and are, therefore, more likely to reduce the commitment of others to the program.

A further reason for an institutional approach is that some problems in clinical practice arise from interpersonal difficulties that may or may not be cross-cultural. Valuing diversity workshops that are highly interactive among participants provide excellent opportunities for coworkers to get to know each other better and, more importantly, to generate the problem-solving experience necessary to work out future complications. This aspect of diversity training is closely related to a second common approach to cultural competence: sessions in managing diversity.

Managing diversity gets its name from R. Roosevelt Thomas Jr. (1990). As the name implies, these workshops are designed for managers. They also are generic in that the same set of communication and management skills is relevant across a variety of settings, including settings in health care agencies. The Thomas perspective on managing diversity is that success in this area

serves a business bottom line: recognizing that profit is more likely when multicultural creativity is available. Thomas argues that affirmative action is a stopgap along the way to a multicultural workplace; simply valuing diversity is not enough. Instead, managing diversity ensures that the diversity that constitutes the American population, and that also is seen in an increasingly more global marketplace, is fully integrated into the workplace.

The topics included in managing diversity workshops are likely to be identical with any kind of management training, with the exception that all of the information and exercises are aimed at cultural and other diversity issues. Thus, a core feature of managing diversity workshops will be an understanding of ethnocentrism and related prejudices that restrict one's ability to be flexible. In addition, there is likely to be culture-by-culture information about, for example, the religious or family practices of various ethnic groups. As Thomas (1990) explained, Willie Mays rarely caught the ball "correctly," but he sure caught the ball. Given the theme of flexibility, other topics might include:

- Communication Skills

- Conflict Resolution Skills

- Multicultural Creativity

The combination of valuing diversity and managing diversity provides an excellent baseline for a hospital, other health care agency, or school of nursing. These workshops, which can span three days, offer the opportunity for coworkers to talk and explore their differences and similarities. In addition, various exercises (e.g., the "cultural bump," in which participants discuss occasions when ignorance of a cultural pattern has caused problems in interpersonal relations), simulations (e.g., "Bafa, Bafa"; see Bafa Bafa, Hummel and Peters, and

Shirts entries in Suggested Readings and Resources, section 9) and/or videos (e.g., Tale of "O"; see Kanter entry in Suggested Readings and Resources, section 9) can enhance people' s abilities to identify with the consequences of difference and of prejudice for other individuals. Managing diversity sessions strengthen leaders' abilities to foster and maintain the gains made in coworker sessions.

Clinical Programs

Another type of cultural training activity for health practitioners can be called "clinical cultural competence" or "culturally congruent care." This is where the paradigm shift must really take place — practitioners can be influenced by these clinical workshops or courses to begin the process of thinking differently about their care of patients. Historically, the academic foundations of this topic can be found in schools of nursing that have had required courses, elective courses, "curriculum threads," and occasional lectures offering knowledge about the beliefs, values, customs, and behaviors of various national ethnic groups and international cultures. There has been some criticism of the "laundry list" approach to cultural competence, in which culture after culture is routinely described in more or less detail, often by clinician members of the particular cultural group, since cognitive information does not necessarily change behavior or attitudes. Nonetheless, such an approach to the subject is seen as a beginning and has become an important staple in nursing curricula and in organizational in-service sessions and conferences. The evolution of nursing knowledge about cultural variation may be traced through the numerous articles and books published on cross-cultural and transcultural nursing since the 1960s (see Suggested Readings and Resources).

Over the years, there also has been a growing sophistication in concepts to aid clinicians in using culturally specific information. Madeleine Leininger (e.g., 1970, 1978, 1991) has been one of the most significant authors among those discussing conceptual approaches to utilizing culturally specific information in nursing practice, though a variety of authors have provided other contributions. Leininger and others who were the earliest to conceptualize cultural competence in health care were educated as anthropologists. These authors (e.g., Chrisman 1981; Kavanagh and Kennedy 1992; Tripp-Reimer 1984) introduced anthropological concepts such as values, beliefs, culture, and ethnocentrism to nursing practice. Currently, the content in nursing courses and cultural competence training sessions is likely to be a synthesis of cultural descriptions, anthropological concepts, and multicultural concepts drawn from a variety of disciplines. We offer four examples here that reflect the most common types of training currently offered across the United States.

The first practitioner, Josepha Campinha-Bacote, is an independent trainer and consultant located in the Midwest who, like other trainers, offers a range of services. For example, her basic workshop builds on a set of three objectives: that participants will be able to (1) define cultural competence; (2) discuss her model of cultural awareness, cultural knowledge, cultural skill, and cultural encounters with others in the group; and (3) identify cultural interventions (Campinha-Bacote 1994). Participants are shown that diversity refers to all of us, and that there is a great deal of intracultural as well as intercultural variation. During the workshop, which can be offered over a 90-minute to eight-hour period, participants interact and reflect on the content and exercises. Content includes an examination of cultural pluralism, frameworks for understanding variation, assessment skills, biological differences, ethnic pharmacology, and culturally specific information. Campinha-Bacote views cultural competence as a journey, rather than as a concrete state that is achieved.

A second example of training is provided by Noel Chrisman, located in the Northwest, who organizes his presentations around what he calls "culture-sensitive care," implying that cultural competence is designed for all clients. The three principles of culture-sensitive care are (1) knowledge (of cultures, of clinical and cultural skills, and of self), (2) mutual respect (between practitioner and client), and (3) negotiation (a technique for meeting clients' needs on their own terms) [Chrisman 1991a, 1991b]. Chrisman's approach is keyed to the everyday activities of practicing nurses, and focuses on the use of the cultural assessment interview (as does the approach of Campinha-Bacote) in the context of the illness-disease distinction, in order to influence practitioners to always listen for cultural perspectives. Chrisman also attempts to help practitioners see the degree to which their own health care system provides hidden cultural perspectives that create barriers to culturally competent care.

A third practitioner offering training is Chuck Pitkofsky, from the West Coast. Pitkofsky's flexible one-day workshop, while incorporating a variation on Campinha-Bacote's approach, is more overtly like diversity training than either of the examples above. The seven components of his workshop include (1) an introduction, in which people make cultural introductions and set group norms; (2) key concepts, such as culture, ethnocentrism, cultural relativity, and cultural competence; (3) stereotypes and their effects on care; (4) cross-cultural communication, including working with interpreters; (5) conflict resolution; (6) relations between the organization and the

community; and (7) a conclusion, in which participants design and commit to personal action plans. Like other practitioners, including the example cited next, Pitkofsky (1995) attempts to help institutions identify internal expertise for understanding specific cultures and set up a diversity task force.

A final example of the kinds of cultural awareness training offered to health care organizations is Kathryn Kavanagh's approach in the East. She carefully shapes her workshops to fit the specific needs of the audience, and discusses the necessary knowledge, attitudes, and skills for dealing with the many sources of diversity in the United States. The conceptual core of one of her basic presentations includes a contrast between "natural bias" and "negative bias" in the conduct of observations and information processing. The latter includes stereotyping and leads to discriminatory behaviors, while the former uses generalizations and can culminate in open client relationships. Leininger's interventions, such as "cultural care preservation" (Leininger 1991), are recommended, as are the "concernful practices" described by Diekelmann (1990). In addition to attending to the range of professional attributes needed by the competent nurse — such as sensitivity to cultural issues, the ability to take action, and information about issues — Kavanagh stimulates listeners to identify and discuss whether these attributes are present in their organizations and communities (Kavanagh and Kennedy 1992).

Interprofessional Cultural Training

The institutional approach to training offered in this chapter also encompasses workshops that focus on organization supports, as well as on practitioners and others meeting the public. For example, one of the key problems facing schools of nursing is ensuring that student cultural competence is reinforced throughout the curriculum. In addition to curricular policy recommendations (cf., Chrisman 1995), special faculty development opportunities may be offered. DeSantis (1991) describes one such project in which cultural understanding in clinical and research settings is stressed through the use of anthropological concepts and methods. Chrisman recently experimented with another model in which faculty were shown ways to integrate cultural concepts into classroom and clinical settings in order to reinforce cultural competence that had been taught in other sectors of the curriculum. As in the DeSantis model, faculty learned to use typical analytic concepts, but also used seminar time to integrate personal "cultural immersion" experiences (a requirement) with diversity training (attended by all faculty) and personal clinical experiences. The most productive aspect of the Chrisman course involved problem-solving discussions relevant to specific clinical cases.

Another type of in-service session or workshop that can contribute to positive interpersonal relationships might be called interprofessional cultural training. Built on a foundation of valuing and managing diversity, these brief interventions can help attune health care professionals to the cultural differences among themselves, and can offer tools and techniques for working across professions, thereby strengthening organizational infrastructure. For example, home care social workers must obtain referrals through nurses, yet they may not understand how to present their skills to nurses so that referrals can be well-managed and reimbursed. Personal resentments may be produced when these preventable misunderstandings occur. Interprofessional cultural training offers a framework for facilitating interdisciplinary relations in environments that demand teamwork

(Tresolini and Pew-Fetzer Task Force 1994).

Finally, there are workshops for trustees and administrators on organizational cultural competence. Our stress on a whole institution approach requires that there be top-down support and leadership. Workshops for leaders must include joint visions, goals, and mission setting so that overall directions can be created. These directions, of course, must include culturally appropriate care. Specific means for implementing goals should include a broad-based hiring, retention, and promotion plan, as well as the kinds of training that are discussed herein. It is appropriate that our concern with culture in this chapter includes the explicit goal of changing organizational culture as part of the achievement of institutional cultural competence. [See Cross et al. 1989 for a discussion of the elements of organizational cultural competence.] Such broad goals that nonetheless require specific and concerted action provide an excellent focus for continuous quality improvement approaches. Accompanying cultural changes, noticeable structural changes in power relationships are likely to occur, supporting the same goals as the other training approaches.

The Organization as a Whole

Workshops and conferences covering the topics and approaches described in this chapter must take place within an institutional context that will support a continuity of personal and group efforts. Piecemeal in-service sessions or workshops may not build the necessary threshold or critical mass for the participants themselves to maintain cultural competence. For this to happen, institutional approaches are necessary. The following brief description of one institutional approach, which is used at Harborview Medical Center in Seattle, is presented here in order to illustrate the kinds of factors involved, to provide the sense that such a project can be accomplished, and to stimulate readers to discover similarities in their own regions or cities.

Harborview is an internationally known trauma center, and is a key resource for most immigrant, refugee, and minority groups of the city in which it is located. Thus, it has an extremely diverse population. At the macro level, this hospital's mission and goals include a statement about poor and underserved members of society, a statement that has allowed its nurses to focus on cultural differences. Moreover, clinicians across the institution have adopted patient-oriented care as a practice framework, allowing further attention to cultural differences in care. These qualities, along with backing from the hospital administration, provide a hospital-wide foundation for more circumscribed projects, such as the cross-cultural training instituted by nursing services. In this case, the theoretical and skill content of the available training replicates that of the training presented earlier in this chapter. The process is equally important.

To achieve long-term commitment, Mich (1995) used strategies from community organizations to implement cultural competence training in this particular setting. Her assessment ranged across the hospital, generating a list of existing resources, and, just as important, creating interactive ties among disparate projects. Training occurred unit by unit and was guided by nurses, so that the timing and style of delivery could be adjusted to the needs of the nurse consumers. In addition, success in one unit stimulated interest among subsequent groups of nurses. Finally, each unit chose one ethnic group that was strongly represented in its population. This allowed a relevant cultural example to be chosen, and for links to be created with leaders within that group, opening up the boundaries between hospital and community. [For a similar example in Minneapolis, see Spring et al. 1995.]

Conclusion

This brief review has revealed that a wide range of training activities in cultural competence is being carried out among a variety of institutions throughout the United States. While we have outlined some exemplars, we certainly have not exhausted the possibilities. Additionally, while we have presented some of the innovation and creativity occurring in a few geographic areas, readers should recognize that such activities are happening all over the country. There is a growing cadre of academics and trainers whose work is becoming more sophisticated and who are available in cities and towns in virtually all parts of the country.

Summary of Issues

1. Current training programs tend to be piecemeal, fragmented efforts to address cultural competence in both health services and educational organizations.

2. Current training programs frequently do not include all staff and managers.

3. Knowledge and skill expectations are inconsistently maintained throughout organizations.

4. There is incomplete conceptualization with respect to the nature of cultural competence.

5. Many current training programs tend to emphasize racial and/or ethnic diversity with little attention to other differences and to the social structures that perpetuate discrimination.

6. There is virtually no research on cultural training.

Recommended Strategies

1. Specify the elements desired in a comprehensive training program before hiring a consultant or designing a series of workshops.

2. Board members and executives of health services agencies and schools of nursing must commit their organizations to adopting and implementing both cultural training and structural change in order to infuse cultural competence throughout all units.

3. Participation in cultural training will be mandatory for all managers, clinicians, staff, faculty, and students.

4. Scholars will develop consensus on the conceptualization of cultural competence and will create a variety of theoretical frameworks to concretely guide nursing actions.

5. Cultural training will illuminate how all types of institutional discrimination are perpetuated by pervasive power differentials, uneven distribution of resources, and elitist practices.

6. Nurse researchers will collaborate on a program of research leading to appropriate evaluative testing of cross-cultural nursing interventions for various populations and nursing specialties, and will develop suitable training mechanisms.

Preferred Outcomes

1. Training programs will be comprehensive and coupled with institutional alignment of mission, structure, and culture.

2. All members of the organization will be trained and oriented to the knowledge, skills, and actions needed for culturally competent practice.

3. Members of organizations will adopt a theoretical framework to guide the conceptualization, integration, and coordination of their cultural transformation efforts.

4. Over time, power in organizations will be shared more widely and will be less distributed by hierarchical position and elitist tradition.

5. Health services research and program evaluations will guide the design and assessment of cultural training.

6. There is evidence of interprofessional and interpersonal harmony and productive work activity among all members of educational and health services organizations.

References

Campinha-Bacote, J. 1994. Cultural competence in psychiatric-mental health nursing: A conceptual model. Nursing Clinics of North America 29 (1): 8-11.

Chrisman, N.J. 1981. Nursing in the context of social and cultural systems. In Concepts basic to nursing, 3rd ed., eds. P.H. Mitchell and A. Loustau, pp. 37-52. New York: McGraw-Hill.

———. 1991a. Cultural systems. In Cancer nursing: A comprehensive textbook, eds. S. Baird, R. McCorkle, and M. Grant, pp. 45-54. Philadelphia: W.B. Saunders.

———. 1991b. Culture-sensitive nursing care. In Medical-surgical nursing: Pathophysiologic concepts, 2nd ed., eds. M. Patrick, S. Woods, R. Craven, J. Rokosky, and P. Bruno, pp. 34-46. Philadelphia: J.B. Lippincott.

———. 1995. Guest editorial. Why transcultural/multicultural course(s) are necessary undergraduate requirements. Journal of Multicultural Nursing and Health 1 (3): 6-7.

Cross, T.L.; Bazron, B.J.; Dennis, K.W.; and Isaacs, M.R. 1989. Toward a culturally competent system of care, vol. I. Washington, D.C.: Child and Adolescent Service System Program, Georgetown University.

DeSantis, L. 1991. Developing faculty expertise in culturally focused care and research. Journal of Professional Nursing 7 (5): 300-309.

Diekelmann, N. 1990. Nursing education: Caring, dialogue, and practice. Journal of Nursing Education 29 (7): 300-305.

Eisenberg, D.M.; Kessler, R.C.; Foster, C.; Norlock, F.E.; Calkins, D.R.; and Delbanco, T.L. 1993. Unconventional medicine in the United States: Prevalence, costs, and patterns of use. New England Journal of Medicine 328 (4): 246-252.

Kavanagh, K.H. and Kennedy, P.H. 1992. Promoting cultural diversity: Strategies for health care professionals. Newbury Park, Calif.: Sage.

Leininger, M.M. 1970. Nursing and anthropology: Two worlds to blend. New York: John Wiley & Sons.

———. 1978. Transcultural nursing: Concepts, theories, and practices. New York: John Wiley & Sons.

———, ed. 1991. Culture care diversity and universality: A theory of nursing. New York: National League for Nursing.

Lenburg, C.B.; Lipson, J.G.; Demi, A.S.; Blaney, D.R.; Stern, P.N.; Schultz, P.R.; and Gage, L. 1995. Promoting cultural competence in and through nursing education: A critical review and comprehensive plan for action. Washington, D.C.: American Academy of Nursing.

Mich, M.K. 1995. Assessment of cultural competence and recommendations for advances at Harborview Medical Center. Master's thesis, University of Washington.

O'Neil, E.H. 1993. Health professions education for the future: Schools in service to the nation. San Francisco: The Pew Health Professions Commission.

Pederson, P. 1988. A handbook for developing multicultural awareness. Alexandria, Va.: American Association for Counseling and Development.

Pitkofsky, C. Personal communication with N. Chrisman, February 16, 1995.

Shugars, D.A.; O'Neil, E.H.; and Bader, J.D., eds. 1991. Healthy America: Practitioners for 2005, an agenda for action for U.S. health professional schools. Durham, N.C.: The Pew Health Professions Commission.

Spring, M.A.; Ross, P.J.; Etkin, N.L.; and Deinard, A.S. 1995. Sociocultural factors in the use of prenatal care by Hmong women. American Journal of Public Health 85 (7): 1015-1017.

Thomas Jr., R.R. 1990. From affirmative action to affirming diversity. Harvard Business Review 68 (2): 107-118.

Tresolini, C.P. and the Pew-Fetzer Task Force. 1994. Health professions education and relationship-centered care. San Francisco: The Pew Health Professions Commission.

Tripp-Reimer, T. 1984. Cultural assessment. In Nursing assessment: A multidimensional approach, eds. J. Bellack and P. Bamford, pp. 226-246. Monterey, Calif.: Wadsworth Health Sciences.

Zola, I.K. 1972. Studying the decision to see a doctor. Advances in Psychosomatic Medicine 8: 216-236.

---

[0] Some material for this section was gathered through the "Nursing and Culture" Internet discussion group, GLOBALRN, supervised by Chuck Pitkofsky (globalrn@itssrv1.ucsf.edu). Electronic communications offer numerous opportunities for national and international discussions of culture and diversity.

Chapter 10

*Building for the Future:
Strategies to Enhance
Cultural Sensitivity*

Cheryl B. Stetler, PhD, RN, FAAN
Jacqueline A. Dienemann, PhD, RN,
CNAA, FAAN

The underlying theme of this monograph is that we in nursing, like others in our society, have work to do to enhance cultural sensitivity, both among ourselves as caregivers and in our caregiving relationships with clients from a wide variety of cultures. In this last chapter, a presentation of strategies currently in use within educational and practice settings indicates that efforts are indeed underway in the profession to achieve this goal of cultural sensitivity. The examples presented herein were submitted in response to an open call for "success stories" through The American Nurse and the AONE News Update in the fall of 1995. Although many of the strategies follow familiar methods, it is hoped that by sharing them others will find ideas that can enhance cultural competence within their own health care settings.

The success stories will be presented in one of two formats: as either an individual case description within the text or as part of the tables at the end of this chapter. The cases include examples from clinical settings and academia. The authors' own words were used to construct both formats. Within the summary tables, stories are organized around one of the following topics:

- strategies designed to enhance the sensitivity of future caregivers through a focus on students and/or faculty;

- strategies designed to enhance the sensitivity of current caregivers; or

- new roles, systems, and relationships in the practice setting that are designed to improve the provision of culturally sensitive care.

To further strengthen the value of this chapter, two sets of observations will be shared: a brief section on "Lessons Learned" by those who created and instituted the strategies outlined in the success stories, and "Questions for Nurses Administrators" on the state of the art of culturally sensitive care by the two authors of this chapter. For the purpose of initiating discussion and debate, the latter questions will be generated from the content of the success stories *as if* they represented the current approach of educational and practice organizations to the issue of cultural diversity. In doing so, it must be noted that the observations *do not* reflect upon the approach of any of the organizations highlighted in the success stories. While all authors were concerned enough about this aspect of nursing to initiate a strategy and interested enough to share some aspect of their work and success with colleagues, they were not asked to provide complete descriptions of their organizations' approaches to this difficult issue. Therefore, the identified issues and provocative dialogue should in no way be considered a negative reflection upon these efforts and their related outcomes.

Case #1: Beth Israel Medical Center[0]

The organizational philosophy of Beth Israel Medical Center is that employee diversity is not only to be recognized, but to be valued. The organization has an extremely diverse staff and patient population, and is committed to creating an environment where all employees — regardless of race, gender, religion, or sexual orientation — can grow and succeed. If such diversity is ignored and organizational values are not honored, it is assumed that both job satisfaction and productivity are decreased.

Early in 1991, the administration looked at incidents such as hate crimes and bias that were occurring in the immediate vicinity, and chose to be proactive before similar incidents began to occur within the medical center. The result was a collaboration with the Anti-Defamation League of B'nai B'rith to present a program entitled "A Workplace of Difference." All employees, including top management, were required to attend this dynamic program, and over 3,500 individuals have done so since April 1991.

The highly interactive program includes small group exercises, a cultural simulation exercise, and video vignettes that present subtle scenes of prejudice and discrimination. The program's goals are for each participant to:

- critically examine stereotypes and assumptions,

- increase awareness of individual attitudes and assumptions,

- appreciate commonalties among different cultures,

- identify strategies to deal with diversity issues, and

- identify enriching aspects of diversity in the workplace.

Participants are encouraged to look at their own heritages, and to identify and share these heritages with others. They also take an exam to assess their knowledge of prominent people from different cultural and religious backgrounds; the results of this exam usually show how little we know about people who are different from ourselves. Of particular note is the continual focus on how content relates to the workplace and on two basic diversity skills: (1)

the ability and willingness to ask questions, and (2) the ability and willingness to give answers. Managers are given the additional challenge of creating an environment in which these skills can flourish.

Participation in the program is now a required part of new employee orientation, intended to promote at the onset of employment the attitude that Beth Israel Medical Center is a diverse workplace where discrimination is not an acceptable behavior. The program is always presented by two trainers, themselves Beth Israel employees, who represent different ethnic and/or cultural backgrounds. This allows for better content facilitation and decreases the possibility of resistance or backlash.

Evaluations have been excellent; in fact, word of mouth has been so positive that employees have asked to attend. Subsequently, the medical center also has incorporated cultural considerations into many of its other programs, such as preceptor workshops, patient education programs, and pain management rounds.

Case #2: Indiana University School of Nursing[o]

In order to increase an awareness of and sensitivity to the different beliefs and practices of diverse subpopulations within the Indiana University School of Nursing, a minority forum series and dialogue sessions were initiated in 1994. The guiding principles used in planning the program were related to beliefs articulated by the minority advisory council in a five-year strategic plan:

- Diversity is a reality.

- There is strength and richness in diversity.

- Culture shapes our beliefs, attitudes, values, and behavior.

- All people deserve dignity and respect.

- All aspects of health and health care are affected by culture.

Although the program was primarily designed for undergraduate students and their faculty, it was not designed for a particular course. Rather, the minority forum series was defined as a broader initiative that has involved faculty, students, and alumni working together to plan each aspect of the program. Some students are required to attend as part of one of their courses, but many participants come voluntarily. The events are open to all students, faculty, staff, and alumni, as well as to community representatives.

Each year, the focus of this dynamic program has changed as follows:

- The first year featured locally and nationally known speakers, such as Drs. Ildora Rhode, Elizabeth Carnegie, Louise Goggans, and Diane Slaughter-DeFoe.

- In the second year, the format involved critical dialogue sessions about the value of diversity, rather than formal presentations. The featured speakers were Drs. Beverly Malone and Annette Dula.

- In its third year, the program expanded to include a series of celebration activities focusing on diversity within and among different subpopulations (e.g., Indo-Europeans, African Americans, Hispanics, Native Americans, and Asian Americans). Each event began with the opportunity to taste cuisine typical of the featured group and, when possible, music, decor, and costumes were used to create the proper ethnic atmosphere. Following the food tasting were presentations by a panel of students, faculty, staff, alumni, and community representatives who were familiar with the health issues affecting that particular subpopulation.

- In the fourth year, the concept of diversity was further expanded to include presentations on the hearing impaired, ageism, gender issues, and biracial/bicultural perspectives.

Attendance at the events over all four years has averaged 75 participants from a variety of ethnic and racial backgrounds. Evaluations collected at the end of each session have been positive, including such comments as: "helpful in understanding how people think and function"; "the format fostered a relaxed and informative atmosphere"; "the concept of 'respect' has been enlarged"; "the sessions stretched my thinking in terms of meeting the needs of patients." Additionally, faculty have invited panel presenters to return and make presentations in specific classes, an indication that concepts are being further integrated into student education.

Case #3: The Women's Ambulatory Care Center of Hartford Hospital and the Hispanic Health Council [o]

The Women's Ambulatory Care Center of Hartford Hospital provides approximately 28,000 patient visits per year to a low-income population that is approximately 67 percent Latino (mostly Puerto Rican), 18 percent African American, 12 percent white, and 3 percent other ethnicities. The Hispanic Health Council is a community-based organization that strives to alter existing inadequacies in the quality and quantity of health care available to the local Hispanic population. In its early years, the Hispanic Health Council viewed Hartford Hospital as a target of its advocacy. As the years progressed, however, both institutions began to initiate collaborations in patient services for the community's Hispanic population, which disproportionately suffers from health problems that include infant mortality, low birthweight, diabetes, asthma, HIV infection, and substance abuse.

Since the mid-1980s, Hartford Hospital and the Hispanic Health Council have worked in partnership on an increasing number of projects, utilizing the strength of each organization to provide high quality care that incorporates consideration of three critical factors:

1. ethnicity and the related diversity of culture,

2. economic class and its related issues, and

3. political/historical circumstances, including the experience of racism.

Hartford Hospital now includes members of the Hispanic Health Council's administration and staff on its board of directors and on committees and other bodies within the institution. In turn, the Hispanic Health Council now has a senior hospital staff member on its board of directors. Together, the two groups have initiated a comprehensive set of strategies that focus on staff, patients, and the community in order to facilitate culturally sensitive care. Five of these strategies are highlighted below:

1. Comadarona Program — The Comadarona Program seeks to link pregnant women with prenatal care, help them stay in care, and assist them in utilizing clinical services successfully. The program includes direct service staff from each organization and ongoing direction and management from program administrators to assist, for example, in the development of mutually established protocols for routine and emergency patient follow-up.

2. Clinic Atabex-Prenatal Services — The goal of this program is to provide care to those women most marginalized from health care (e.g., those who are chemically dependent or mentally ill). Located

in a clinical space at the Hispanic Health Council, services are free, bilingual, and provided by staff from both organizations.

3. Partnership for Health Education — The two organizations have agreed on a plan to break with tradition and incorporate the Hispanic Health Council's Comadarona staff into the Women's Ambulatory Care Center's health education program. This staff, using an agreed-upon curriculum and trained by the center's education coordinator, will provide bilingual health education to patients, in partnership with RNs at the clinic.

4. Patient Focus Groups — Focus groups were held to obtain direct input from patients and were facilitated by bilingual employees outside of the center so that patients would be able to freely share their suggestions for improvement. A written hospital survey, translated into Spanish, also provides ongoing feedback.

5. Staff Cultural Competency Training and Spanish Classes — An outside company evaluated all hospital staff members who expressed interest in language training based on their baseline knowledge of Spanish. Two advanced groups are now being given language instruction 2 1/2 hours per day, two days per week as part of a 10-week program.

Lessons Learned

Success story authors were asked not only to share their goals, interventions, and results, but also to reflect upon what they had learned through this process that might be helpful to their peers. The following testimonials can be of use to administrators, educators, clinicians, and students as they reflect upon their own cultural competence or that of their organization.

- "You don't have to be, or feel, very different to feel like an outsider. As nurses, it is so important to reach out with sensitivity in terms of the patient's level of comfort... so important to bridge that gap and celebrate the uniqueness of each individual we touch" (Mary Hindelang, RN, PhD — see Table 10.3 #1).

- "Do not ignore prejudice or stereotyping when it occurs. Acknowledge resistance — do not ignore it or become defensive. Let people express their feelings. Many of us are afraid of the tension around these issues, but if you do not say anything, you send the message that you are in agreement with such behavior. Tension may be unavoidable, and some of these issues will not disappear without a struggle" (Anne Dickinson Cohen, MA, RNC — see Case #1).

- "It is always best to anticipate what other languages a particular video project will be in prior to initial production. Spanish is about 1/3 longer than English. As a result, our Spanish voice-over had to be extremely fast. In retrospect, the English script should have been written and produced differently to accommodate this difficulty" (Jackie A. Smith, PhD — see Table 10.4 #6).

- "Our strategies of making our workshops mandatory — with the full support of our chief of staff and director of nursing — including cultural competency on our performance evaluations, and giving the line staff themselves the opportunity to become trainers, all worked toward giving our program the importance and relevance it deserved" (Lucy Fisher, RN, MS, CNS, and Jane Goldman, RN, MS — see Table 10.3 #4).

- "There is no quick fix for developing cultural competency. The work must be ongoing and multifaceted. It includes acknowledging that the health care institution operates within its own cultural context and that traditional structures have to be challenged and, in some cases, altered for effective and appropriate care" (Susan Maxwell, MBA, RN, CNA, and Grace Damio, MS — see Case #3).

- "Incorporate content earlier in the curriculum and continue its application to nursing as a thread throughout each course. The process must be both valued and shared by the nursing faculty" (Suzanne Billingsley, RN, MSN, CS; Elena Hall, RN, MSN; and Clarisa Shavers, RN, MS,C — see Table 10.1 #3).

- "If we truly value cultural diversity, then all avenues for sharing and learning have potential. Creativity and collaboration in seeking out these avenues are skills that nurses possess. Using these skills toward cultural competence is of benefit to all of nursing" (Vicki P. Hines-Martin, PhD, RN, CS — see Table 10.3 #2).

- "While classroom/laboratory cultural orientation is important in understanding other cultures, it is at least as important to interact meaningfully with people from that culture. Thus, understanding is based on direct and primary experience in providing care" (Charles Kemp, RN, CRNH — see Table 10.1 #1).

- "Even if you are from the same culture, you still have to overcome prejudices in many things — above all, in illiteracy — in order to be able to teach the patient or class participant. Having the ability to speak the language, you still need to build a trusting relationship with the person and their family to be able to assist in realizing the importance of compliance" (Naomi Aranda Garcia, RN — see Table 10.4 #4).

Questions for Nurse Administrators

As part of their "lessons learned," some of the success story authors discussed issues that nurse administrators, whether in service or education, obviously must begin to address if culturally sensitive care is to become a widespread reality before the next century (e.g., efforts cannot be isolated activities). Based on these lessons, as well as on an analysis of the types of strategies described — or not described — within the 26 success stories, several questions can be posed to administrators in both service and academia:

1. Is culturally sensitive care seen as a "nice to do" or a "need to do" activity?

Many of the activities appeared to be generated by committed individuals or small segments of an overall organization. Such activities presumably were valued, but does the fact that they often appeared to be isolated incidents reflect a lack of commitment on the part of the nurse executive or related power structure?

2. Will creating self-awareness really do the trick?

Many of the programs focused on cultural awareness, an obviously important step toward cultural competence. On the other hand, few stories included reports of skill-based assessments or systematic skill-building activities. Why the lack of such reports? Is there a lack of available skill-building systems that are valid, reliable, and reasonably priced from which administrators can choose? If not, how can they be generated?

3. Are administrators ready to reengineer their current systems?

Few of the stories described a comprehensive approach to the creation of a culturally competent system of care. Only a few examples appeared to systematically convert the value of sensitivity into concrete performance expectations for managers and employees. Without such a fundamental change there cannot, in all likelihood, be widespread operationalism of "culturally competent" organizational beliefs and values. Without a related infrastructure, how can lasting change occur? Part of this infrastructure will include the appointment of managers and other leaders from diverse cultures. Of interest is the fact not one success story was submitted that focused primarily on developing or recruiting such leaders. This need for infrastructure applies equally to academic settings, and thus to performance expectations for faculty. Why, for example, should we assume that educators naturally have or will apply complex skills that have yet to be widely identified?

4. What is the value of a conceptual framework?

Some of the success stories clearly were guided by a conceptual framework; others apparently were not. If we are a scientifically based profession, should there be a guiding conceptual framework for any such organizational effort? To what degree are those frameworks that are available grounded in applied research?

5. What type of data does an administrator need in order to know that progress is being made?

A number of the success stories, at this stage of development, only provided impressionistic or self-reported evaluative information. As implied earlier, self-reported awareness is not the same as validated competencies, nor is it the same as client outcomes. In terms of the latter, a number of practice settings are obtaining patient satisfaction data, an obviously important source of information. However, what is being asked of the patients? Some patient "attitude" questionnaires do not appropriately assess whether patient needs have been adequately met (Gerteis et al. 1993), and some may not provide administrators with information sufficient enough to help make continuous improvements in the area of cultural responsiveness. Of added value are rates of complications, readmissions, and other concrete patient outcomes. Are administrators aware of whether these parameters differ among minority groups? Have they explored whether culturally specific strategies made a difference?

6. Where is the collaboration between service and education?

Most of the reported success stories involve either service or education, but not integrated, collaborative efforts. Are we missing an opportunity to learn together and create strategies that help those entering our profession to learn and then immediately use new skills in reinforcing practice environments?

Conclusion

As Robert Frost's poem so aptly described, we have "miles to go" before we will have widespread cultural competence within the nursing profession, thereby providing a role model to others in society. Nonetheless, we should not ignore the fact that successful efforts are being implemented within both academic and practice settings. Ongoing communication from the success story authors indicates that a number are expanding their successful efforts and that additional activities to enhance cultural sensitivity are occurring within their organizations. A word of thanks to all of these authors and their colleagues as they enhance the care of diverse patients throughout the country.

References

Gerteis, M.; Edgman-Levitan, S.; Daley, J.; and Delbanco, T. 1993. Through the patient's eyes. San Francisco: Jossey-Bass.

[0] Submitted by Anne Dickinson Cohen, MA, RNC/Staff Development Coordinator/Nursing Education and Research/Beth Israel Medical Center/First Avenue at 16th Street/New York, NY 10003.

[0] Submitted by Lillian Stokes, RN, MSN, PhD/Associate Professor and Co-Chair, Minority Advisory Council, and Robyn Gibboney, MA, PhD/Executive Assistant to University Dean/Indiana University School of Nursing/1111 Middle Drive/Indianapolis, IN 46202.

[0] Submitted by Susan Maxwell, MBA, RN, CNA/Nurse Manager, and Grace Damio, MS/Coordinator of Maternal and Child Health Unit/Hartford Hospital/80 Seymour Street/Hartford, CT 06102.

Table 10.1

Enhancing the Sensitivity of Future Caregivers, through a Focus on Nursing Students

Setting/Authors	Populations	Goals	Interventions/Strategies

1. Baylor University, School of Nursing, 3700 Worth Street, Dallas, TX 75246.
 	
Charles Kemp, RN, CRNH, Clinical Instructor.
	Students: undergraduate; primarily white, middle-class, and Protestant.
	
	Clients: refugees from, for example, Cambodia, Vietnam, Laos, and Kurdistan.
		Increase an understanding of both the culture of origin and the common culture of experience (i.e., refugee) in order to better meet patients' health care needs.	Focus on studying with patient populations, rather than studying about them, by providing services according to their expressed needs:
			• Learn directly from the population about who they are and what they need, rather than from health care or refugee service providers.
			• In the process of providing services, begin the development of a data base on health care beliefs and practices, as well as on barriers to health care.
			• Day 1 of clinical: 8-hour workshop is held on cultural characteristics and health care beliefs/practices of target populations:
			  ☞ demonstrate and discuss traditional health practices and medicines,
			  ☞ use films and handouts.
			• Day 2 of clinical: each two-person team of students is introduced to one or two families referred from the previous semester:
			  ☞ while spending time with families, assess their past and current problems
			  ☞ begin work to address identified problems;
			• After several hours in the community, students help to plan for the remainder of the semester.
			• Overall, students provide primary care to individuals and families, help to provide community care services such as mammography, and educate families about health.

Table 10.1 - continued
Enhancing the Sensitivity of Future Caregivers, through a Focus on Nursing Students

Setting/Authors	Populations	Goals	Interventions/Strategies
2. Central Connecticut State University, Dept. of Health and Human Service Professions, 1615 Stanley Street, P.O. Box 4010, New Britain, CT 06050-4010. Faculty members *Mary Jane Williams, PhD, RN; Nancy Organek, PhD, RN; and Linda Barile, PhD, RN; and Judith Hriceniak,*	*PhD, RN, Chair.*	**Students:** RN undergraduate; primarily white and female. **Clients:** in acute care rehabilitation across the continuum; from urban areas. Increase awareness of issues related to diversity.	Introduction of concepts within course on theoretical foundations: • definition of culture and transcultural nursing, per Leininger[1]; • examination of students' values and related impact on professional behavior; • analysis of culture and its effect on a person's level of wellness, interaction with the health care system, and relationship with the nurse; • discussion of effects of culture on the nursing process; • examination of relevant research; • assignment to write a paper on a specific cultural habit and present content to peers. Application of concepts in other theoretical areas, across the curriculum.
Setting/Authors	**Populations**	**Goals**	**Interventions/Strategies**
3. Henry Ford Hospital School of Nursing, 2921 West Grand Boulevard, Detroit, MI 48202. Instructors *Suzanne Billingsley, RN, MSN, CS; Elena Hall, RN, MSN; and Clarisa Shavers, RN, MS,C.*	**Students:** undergraduate; mostly white females from suburbs. **Clients:** African Americans, Asians/Orientals, Hispanics/ Mexican Americans, Arabs/Mediterraneans, and whites; from urban and surburban areas.	Increase awareness of bias and stereotyping; of cultural differences as they influence traditions, values, beliefs and health practices; and of culturally appropriate care. Lessen tensions related to cultural interactions among students and with patients.	Clinical conferences over one month's time: • resources = Leininger and Rokeach[2]; • assigned readings addressing how cultural practices affect behavior and health care; • discussion of own cultural heritage and the current impact it has on one's life; • experiential learning simulation to help understand what it is like to be seen as "different" or treated with insensitivity (i.e., students are divided into cultural groups and follow a set of unequal, but subtle, norms for one clinical day); • case studies for application of cultural concepts to patient care management.

[1] M. Leininger, *Culture Care Diversity and Universality: A Theory of Nursing*, New York: National League of Nursing, 1991.
[2] M. Rokeach, *Beliefs, Attitudes and Values*, San Francisco: Jossey-Bass, 1968.

Setting/Authors	Populations	Goals	Interventions/Strategies
4. Iowa Central Community College, Division of Health Sciences, Ave. M, Fort Dodge, IA 50501. *Susan K. Zupan[3], RNC, Instructor and Migrant Nurse for Proteus Employment Opportunities.*	**Students:** undergraduate; primarily of Northern European descent living in rural areas; two African Americans. **Clients:** migrants of Mexican descent.	Help students develop culturally sensitive nursing practice.	Elective in migrant health, in last clinical rotation, to practice the provision of health services to farm workers and their families in homes, stores, and work sites in rural Iowa via a mobile clinic (during "home clinics," Mexican families living in the community invite migrant families to their homes to receive health services); specific activities include: • readings about cultural differences, discussion of case studies, and role-playing implementation of care; • orientation to the mobile health clinic; • practicing of new communication skills and new approaches to health care; • preparation of the van and then patient care (e.g., health histories, physical assessments, and health promotion activities or referrals), including the use of an interpreter, as needed; • use of a student log of activities and interactions, reflection on behavior/attitudes, evaluation of care provided, and recommendations for future rotations; • unplanned time with interpreters, which enabled valuable discussions to take place.

[3] For networking purposes, Ms. Zupan can be contacted at the Central New Jersey Maternal and Child Health Consortium, 501 Hoes Lane, Suite 206, Piscataway, New Jersey 08854, where she is currently a perinatal consultant.

Table 10.1 - continued

Enhancing the Sensitivity of Future Caregivers, through a Focus on Nursing Students

Setting/Authors	Populations	Goals	Interventions/Strategies

5. South Dakota State University, College of Nursing, Box 2275, Brookings, SD 57007.
 	
Patriciann Furnari Brady, EdD, RN, Asst. Professor.
	Students: undergraduate; from a mostly rural pioneer community of predominately German backgrounds.
	
	Clients: pre-dominantly of German or Scandanavian backgrounds.
		Enable a recognition of the effects of students' own culture on their perceptions of self, health beliefs, and nursing practice.	Within the junior-level mental health nursing course:
			• utilization of concept of the therapeutic use of self;
			• completion by students of a broad-based literature review on their cultural backgrounds;
			• completion/summary/analysis of a cultural assessment regarding culture and social structure dimensions that depict caring, health beliefs, and related practices:
			  ☛ by the students of their own personal opinions,
			  ☛ through an interview of an elderly family member,
			  ☛ through an interview of an older member of the community in the student's region.

Table 10.1 - continued

Enhancing the Sensitivity of Future Caregivers, through a Focus on Nursing Students

Setting/Authors	Populations	Goals	Interventions/Strategies
6. Southwestern College, Department of Nursing, 100 College Street, Winfield, KS 67156-2499. *Jane Schlickau, MN, RN, ARNP/CNS, Asst. Professor.*	**Students:** under-graduate; middle-class whites. **Clients:** Hispanic and Vietnamese families.	Allow students to apply their newly acquired, course-related nursing skills in a multicul-tural setting.	Intense, one-week elective rural nursing practicum at end of junior year: • 32 hours of clinical laboratory conducted in agencies such as local health department, local hospital, and Western Kansas Mexican American Ministries Health Clinic; • supervision by a preceptor compe-tent in transcultural nursing; • adaptation of Kolb's[4] experiential learning theory • self-directed learning; • first clinical day, observe and ask as many questions as possible; second clinical day, share various experi-ences in informal classroom; third day, review literature about transcul-tural nursing, continue observations, and prepare to share observations that were validated in the literature; fourth day, continue the above activities and finalize assignments through which outcomes of the experience could be shared with others; • preparation of a group poster for presentation to all nursing students during orientation day at the begin-ning of fall semester; group also prepared a pamphlet describing their practicum experiences in being mentored by nurses competent in transcultural nursing.

[4] D.A.Kolb, *Experinatial Learning*, Englewood Cliffs, NJ: Prentice Hall, 1984.

Table 10.1 - continued
Enhancing the Sensitivity of Future Caregivers, through a Focus on Nursing Students

Setting/Authors	Populations	Goals	Interventions/Strategies
7. Texas Woman's University, College of Nursing, P.O. Box 425498, Denton, TX 76204-3498. *Sally Northam, PhD, RN, Assistant Professor.*	**Students:** graduate and under-graduate. **Clients:** under-served, impoverished individuals of various ethnic backgrounds, including Hispanics, African Americans, Native Americans, Asian Americans, and whites; also, patients in remote rural communities.	Augment the cultural competence of university students while also serving the needs of local impoverished individuals.	Within the nurse-managed TWU C.A.R.E.S. Health Center (Community Assessment Referral and Education Services), located within a low-income housing project, and a related rural outreach program: • exploration of community needs and methods of responding to those expressed needs (i.e., used a needs assessment interview and survey to evaluate health care access among local individuals [see Aday and Anderson[5]]; and utilized items in a health needs assessment survey from the U.S. Depart-ment of Health and Human Services' Hispanic Health and Nutrition Examination Survey[6]); • assessment of the impact of an individual's culture on health beliefs and practices, e.g.: recognition of "fatalismo," and "familismo," and recognition of culture as more than only ethnicity, as with individuals drawn together based on common sexual preferences or age • based on input from the community: hired a Spanish-speaking, Hispanic nurse; offer classes in Spanish, e.g., on parenting; and staff clinic with nurse practitioners to augment ability to treat mild acute illness; • special attention paid to hiring African American and Hispanic university students for dental clinic and nurse-managed clinic • maintenance of a list of interpreters, accessed as needed to interpret and function as client advocates; • utilization of local ethnic festivals to disseminate information about available health services; • provision of role modeling for a variety of students in cultural competence.

[5] L. Aday and R. Anderson, "Equity of Access to Medical Care: A Conceptual and Empirical Overview," *Medical Care* 19 (1981): 4–27
[6] HANES III

Table 10.1 - continued
Enhancing the Sensitivity of Future Caregivers, through a Focus on Nursing Students

Setting/Authors	Populations	Goals	Interventions/Strategies
8. University of North Dakota, College of Nursing, Box 9025, Grand Forks, ND 58202. *Elizabeth Tyree, MPH, RN, Clinical Assoc. Professor; Susan J. Henly, PhD, Assoc. Professor; and Deborah Lindsey, MS, Evaluation Coordinator.*	**Students:** graduate; and undergraduate, enrolled in "Family in the Community" and "Community Health Nursing" courses. **Clients:** from rural cultures, living in poverty, including Native Americans and migrant farm workers.	Prepare nurses to practice in underserved areas and /or with underserved populations. Address the need for access to primary health care among residents of North Dakota and northwestern Minnesota.	Population specific, Nursing Center for Vulnerable Rural Groups: • a nursing center "without walls," with a case management model of service; • reflects a preference for the integration of teaching and service in higher education for health professionals ; • reflects an ecological perspective on the care of individuals in the context of family in the community, which is easily adapted for cultural variation; • clinical assignments carefully selected to maximize student experiences with a wide range of sociocultural groups; • periodic cultural self-assessment encouraged; • use of a data system that includes client demographic data and encounter information to facilitate; the tracking of client services on a semester-by-semester basis.

Table 10.2
Enhancing the Sensitivity of Future Caregivers, through a Focus on Nursing Faculty, Students, and Relevant Others

Setting/Authors	Populations	Goals	Interventions/Strategies
1. East Central University, Department of Nursing, 1000 E. 14th Street, Ada, OK 74820-6899. *Elizabeth Schmelling, PhD,RN,C, Prof. and Chair; Anne Davis, PhD, RN,C, Assoc. Prof.; Judy Parker, PhD, RN,C, Assoc. Prof.; and Deborah Flowers, MS, RN, Instructor.*	**Faculty:** mostly urban; only one is a Native American. **Students:** come from rural areas; approximately 30% are Native Americans.	To help all nursing faculty engaged in clinical instruction: • better understand the concept of culture and traits common to cultural groups represented by their student body; • acquire techniques useful in working with these students.	Inclusion in the faculty manual of a brief, concise section on "Cultural Competence in Clinical Instruction": • written by the Native American faculty member, a legislator of the Chickasaw Nation; • includes a brief introduction to "culture" as a general concept; • emphasizes the need to be aware of cultural differences; • includes suggestions on how to identify misunderstandings and breakdowns in communication related to cultural differences between faculty and students, among students, and between students and clients.
Setting/Authors	**Populations**	**Goals**	**Interventions/Strategies**

2. University of Massachusetts-Lowell, Department of Nursing, One University Ave., Lowell, MA 01854.
 	
Patricia A. Tyra, EdD, RN, CS, Professor; and Carole W. Pearce, PhD, RN,C, Assistant Professor.
	Faculty: College of Health Professions; primarily white and middle-class.
	
	Students: include a small minority representation from Cambodia, Vietnam, China, Africa, and India.
		Enhance the knowledge of faculty, students, and staff regarding Southeast Asian family and health care issues and concerns.	Obtained a seed grant from the university's Council on Diversity and Pluralism to fund the following:
			• panel of Southeast Asian health care experts to address noted issues and concerns; focused, for example, on:
			  ☛ common folk medicine practices, such as *cao gio* (coin rubbing), which in the past could result in referral of patients by uninformed professionals for possible child abuse,
			  ☛ herbal teas, soups, and other medicines,
			  ☛ experiences of the panelists in learning within a different culture;
			• visit to a local herbal medicine store to obtain "representative" herbal medicines for panel discussion and classroom use;
			• preparation by the cafeteria of a special recipe cookie and teas for social time at the panel;
			• purchase of herbal medicine books for faculty use and development of an annotated bibliography;
			• development of a lobby display of health care practices and herbal medicines.

Table 10.2 continued
Enhancing the Sensitivity of Future Caregivers, through a Focus on Nursing Faculty, Students, and Relevant Others

Setting/Authors	Populations	Goals	Interventions/Strategies
3. University of North Carolina at Wilmington, School of Nursing, 601 S. College Rd., Wilmington, NC 28403-3297. *Marlene M. Rosenkoetter, RN, PhD, FAAN, Professor; and Betty J. Reynolds, RN, EdD, Retired Assoc. Professor.*	**Faculty:** **Students:** undergraduate and graduate. **Others:** staff and members of the greater community of Southeastern North Carolina. **Clients:** Native Americans.	Increase knowledge about the culture of Native Americans in order to provide appropriate care within the health care system and build community awareness.	A half-day event, "Celebration of the American Indian": • co-sponsored by the School of Nursing, North Carolina Commission of Indian Affairs, and Coastal Area Health Education Center; • widespread publicity and attendance (600+); • concurrent sessions, repeated to enable broader participation (e.g., music and dance, with an emphasis on the interrelationship of man, nature, and symbolism, plus sessions on history, medicine and folklore, crafts, and customs as presented by Native American and other known experts); • Native American foods available for purchase; • representatives from tribes in native dress • display of crafts and historical items.
Setting/Authors	Populations	Goals	Interventions/Strategies
4. University of Wisconsin-Eau Claire, School of Nursing, Eau Claire, WI 54602-4004. *Susan Diemert Moch, PhD, RN, Assoc. Professor; Geraldine L. Long, MSN, RN, Asst. Professor/Parish Nurse; Josette Wouters Jones, RN, Instructor/ Coordina-tor; Karen Solheim, MS, RN, Asst. Professor/NP; and Kathleen Shadick, MSN, RN, FNP.*	**Faculty:** recruited for the program; predominantly white and middle-class. **Students:** recruited for the program; undergraduate; predominantly white and middle-class. **Clients:** Hmong refugees from Laos in a white semi-rural community.	Learn more about the Hmong culture. For Hmong families, learn about health care within the Western culture.	Health promotion classes: • held at a public elementary school; • interpreter = Hmong nursing student; • at the beginning of each session, Hmong participants are told faculty and students want to learn about Hmong culture during the process of teaching health promotion classes; Hmong participants thus encouraged to share stories and experiences about their cultural group; • one series of four classes in the spring; one in the fall; • initially, faculty teamed with students to teach classes; now nursing students plan and teach classes using nursing faculty as consultants; • learn specifics about teaching diverse groups through consultation with cultural group leaders.

Table 10.3
Enhancing the Sensitivity of Current Caregivers

Setting/Authors	Populations	Goals	Interventions/Strategies
1. Keeweenaw Home Nursing and Hospice, 414 Hecla Street, Laurium, MI 49913. *Mary Hindelang, RN, PhD, Education Coordinator; Wanda Kolb, RN, BSN, Administrator; and Diane Tiberg, RN, Director of Nurses.*	**Staff:** many employees and volunteers from the same cultural background as their clients. **Clients:** rural community; predominantly Finnish.	Provide special attention to the cultural differences of clients, especially the elderly, in this strongly ethnic community	Provision of culturally competent home care through the following: • intensive educational programs for all staff and volunteers at the inception of the hospice program, focusing on the importance of pain assessment, interpretation of non-verbal cues, and understanding of variations in the cultural expression of emotions in this often stoic and polite population, • use of employees and volunteers who speak Finnish; especially helpful with dementia and hospice patients who revert to communicating only in their native tongue in their final stages, • encouragment of culturally sensitive actions (e.g., enabling patients to take a soothing sauna, and celebration of Juhannus Day, an important feast day for many Finns).
Setting/Authors	**Populations**	**Goals**	**Interventions/Strategies**
2. Kyanna Black Nurses Association; University of Kentucky College of Nursing, Psych-Mental Health Division; and Kentucky Nurses Association. Vicki P. Hines-Martin, PhD, RN, CS, Asst. Professor and Immediate Past President, Kyanna Black Nurses Assoc. (College of Nursing, Univ. of Kentucky, Chandler Medical Center, Lexington, KY 40536-0232).	**Staff:** nurses licensed in the state of Kentucky; over 97% are white and female.	Begin the sharing of culture-specific information with the nurses of Kentucky. Assist nurses in understanding and appropriately addressing issues that relate to functioning in a culturally diverse world.	Via a collaborative effort, a column was established in *The Kentucky Nurse*, KNA's official publication, which is mailed quarterly to every nurse licensed in Kentucky: • effort reflects Leininger's cultural care diversity and universality model; • title = "Focus on Diversity"; • first issue in fall 1994 outlined the column's purpose, asked for questions from readers, and presented the first topic on why a column such as this benefits nursing; • columns have included specifics about African American and Appalachian populations, the health care needs of these groups, and environmental factors that affect health; • have responded to questions related to cultural issues in the health care workplace; • provide needed cultural references with each column; • some schools of nursing report use of the column as a teaching tool.

Table 10.3 continued
Enhancing the Sensitivity of Current Caregivers

Setting/Authors	Populations	Goals	Interventions/Strategies

3. North Carolina Breast and Cervical Cancer Control Coalition.
 	
Lorna Harris, PhD, RN, Coalition Chairperson and Director, Office of Minority Affairs, School of Nursing, University of North Carolina at Chapel Hill, Chapel Hill, NC 27599-7460.
	Staff: somewhat culturally diverse.
	
	Clients: women, especially those at high risk, including African Americans, Hispanics, Native Americans, and lesbians.
		Provide communication and coordination for individuals and organizations interested in improving access to and quality of breast and cervical cancer screening services.	Education of health professionals regarding breast and cancer screening and how to provide culturally competent screening care:
			• use of the Professional Education Quality Assurance work group, an interdisciplinary group of health professionals;
			• education of physicians, nurses, and radiology technologists about differences and similarities in beliefs and health practices of patients from diverse cultures and backgrounds;
			• provision of workshops and guidelines;
			• provision of handbooks:
			  ☛ material for MDs, NPs, radiology technologists, and staff nurses on breast and cervical health,
			  ☛ describe how to bring these targeted individuals into the system for screening, how to get information out to each population, and how to practice in a culturally appropriate manner in terms of each group's primary fears and concerns (e.g., privacy, stress alleviation, or use of native medicines).

Table 10.3 continued
Enhancing the Sensitivity of Current Caregivers

Setting/Authors	Populations	Goals	Interventions/Strategies
4. San Francisco General Hospital, department of Psychiatry, 7G 14, 1001 Potrero Ave., San Francisco, CA 94110. *Lucy Fisher, RN, MS, CNS, Co-ordinator, Cultural Competence Program; and Jane Goldman, RN, MS, Cultural Diversity Trainer.*	**Staff:** all disciplines and levels within the Department, both clinical and administrative; culturally, racially, and ethnically diverse with issues of differ-ence and power inequities. **Clients:** diverse (e.g., Asians, African Americans, gays/ lesbians, HIV-positive individuals and Latinos).	Improve working and personal relationships among staff and, in turn, increase the quality of care provided to a diverse patient population.	Implementation of a cultural competency program: • 3-hour mandatory training based on Pinderhughes[7] model, which uses a self-disclosure format to explore differ-ences, family-of-origin values, and per-sonal collusion with racism; also exam-ines attitudes and behaviors in the con-text of power and powerlessness; • use of group trainers who lead by example and thus "go first" as they model personal responses to sensi-tive topics of race, gender, and power; these selected, culturally diverse trainers are given a 2-day "train the trainer workshop" and meet monthly for continuous improvement; • inclusion of cultural competence as part of performance criteria for the department.
Setting/Authors	Populations	Goals	Interventions/Strategies
5. University of Wisconsin Hospitals and Clinics, Department of Nursing, F6-169, 600 Highland Ave., Madison, WI 35792. *Ronnie Peterson, RN, MS, Nursing Supervisor.*	**Staff:** health care workers, typically of white European descent. **Students:** large Asian population at the university. **Clients:** multi-cul-tural, with large Hmong and Russian immigrant populations.	Increase knowl-edge and skills of those individuals involved in provid-ing, coordinating, supporting, and supervising health care to persons of diverse cultures.	Creation of the Interdisciplinary Multicultural Patient Care Team (IMPCT), with an advanced practice nurse and chaplain as co-chairs, that: • assesses the related knowledge base/needs of staff throughout the hospital; • conducts an ongoing review of liter-ature to determine current cultural practices and maintain a related reference list; • hosts an annual Multicultural Awareness Week, with a lecture series, posters, music in waiting areas, and specials in the cafeteria; • develops a resource manual of health and death-related rituals; • creates a resource network of employees with interpretive skills and other useful cultural and religious expertise.

[7] E. Pinderhughes, *Understanding Race, Ethnicity and Power*, New York: The Free Press, 1989.

Table 10.4
New Roles, Systems, and Relationships in the Practice Setting

Setting/Authors	Populations	Goals	Interventions/Strategies
1. Beth Israel Hospital, Nursing Services and Programs, 330 Brookline Ave., Boston, MA 02215.

Eileen C. Hodgman, RN, MSN, FAAN, Project Director and Principal Investigator, Choose Nursing!©

Partner schools: Simmons College, Boston, MA; Salem State College, Salem, MA; and Northeastern University, Boston, MA. | **Students:** Boston public high school; racial/ ethnic minorities and nonminority low-income. | Support students' motivation and capacity to apply to college-based nursing education programs. | *Choose Nursing!©* is a career-oriented preliminary education program designed to:
• identify targeted students with an expressed interest in nursing;
• recruit, select, and enroll a minimum of 15 students completing the 10th grade each year;
• offer over 1,000 hours of hands-on experience, supervision, and one-on-one learning with clinical nurse mentors and patients;
• provide diagnostic academic testing, planning, and remedial/supplemental after-school academics;
• test a competency-based clinical curriculum developed and taught by Beth Israel nurses;
• incorporate college-based workshops to help prepare for college application, admission, and financial aid;
• be disseminated and replicated.

The program exceeded all measurable objectives:
• 107 students applied, 61 enrolled; and 40 graduated over a four-year period;
• all 40 graduates accepted to a four-year college, with students attending 10 different colleges; the first cohort graduates in 1997 and only one student overall has dropped out. |

Setting/Authors	Populations	Goals	Interventions/Strategies
2. The Johns Hopkins Hospital, Department of Nursing, Houck 413, 600 North Wolfe Street, Baltimore, MD 21287. *Carol B. Payne, RN, Nurse Manager, Inpatient Perinatal Unit.*	**Staff:** ethnicity of nursing staff not reflective of patient population. **Clients:** multicultural; primarily African American.	Create an environment of cultural competence; e.g., staff will employ creative strategies to better meet the needs of each individual patient and deliver care in a culturally sensitive and nonjudgmental manner.	Head nurse managerial efforts to create the vision of cultural competence and accommodation: • role modeling of related behaviors: ☞ important to first affirm one's own culture (African American), values, traditions, and beliefs, ☞ important to know oneself, including one's own prejudices; • other strategies: ☞ educating staff, including conferences and articles, ☞ developing special interest activities; e.g., showcase of different cultures on a collage, creation of a flag displaying culture/countries of staff, and implementation of a cultural diversity committee, ☞ recruiting and retaining staff who reflect the community and patient populations, ☞ valuing and highlighting the talent of all staff; e.g., appointing support staff to serve on committees, ☞ encouraging a mentoring relationship between professional and support staff, ☞ maintaining effective communication and a sense of humor, ☞ creating opportunities to share similarities and differences in order to build bonds, ☞ incorporating members of the community into unit activities/programs; e.g., the newborn cuddler program/foster grandparents.
Setting/Authors	**Populations**	**Goals**	**Interventions/Strategies**
3. Mount Sinai Hospital and Medical Center, Division of Diabetes Education, Rm # F-908, 15th & California Ave., Chicago, IL 60608. *Patrick C. Conlon, RN, BSN, CDE, Director, Diabetes Education.*	**Staff:** diverse cultural mix of nursing staff and medical assistants, including African Americans, whites, Filipinos, East Indians, and Latinos. **Clients:** diabetic patients, including African Americans and Latinos, as well as recent Soviet Jewish immigrants.	Establish and maintain a comprehensive instructional support system for those with diabetes, without regard as to race, sex, creed, or ethnic background. Increase the knowledge and skills of staff involved in coordinating diabetes care at the bedside.	A comprehensive, trilingual diabetes intervention program: • creation of culturally sensitive, low literacy educational tools in three languages; • training of staff in Spanish; • group classes in three languages at several times and locations in the community; • contracting with the Mental Health Services for Deaf Adults and Children program (MENDAC) to facilitate assessments to determine the appropriateness for group diabetes sessions or one-on-one diabetes education.

Setting/Authors	Populations	Goals	Interventions/Strategies
4. Northwest Texas Healthcare Systems, Diabetes Center, 1501 South Coulter, Amarillo, TX 79106. *Naomi Aranda Garcia, RN, Diabetes Educator.*	**Clients:** many are Hispanic and have difficulty communicating with caregivers.	Improve communication, care, and self-management for this population, which is currently experiencing high levels of complications.	Bilingual Hispanic nurse who does the following: • holds classes within a local community center where patients feel more comfortable, and collaborates with a bilingual Caucasian dietitian on nutrition classes; • translates materials into down-to-earth Spanish, including colorful flyers; • per the culture, involves the whole family for "self-management" and encouragement; • advertises classes and writes articles in local newspapers, and presents a diabetes talk show on Hispanic radio; • developed a blood glucose monitor fund with the assistance of a Hispanic committee to assist low-income families who have a member with diabetes.
Setting/Authors	**Populations**	**Goals**	**Interventions/Strategies**

5. Northern Arizona University, Nursing Education Center, and Sage Memorial Hospital, P.O. Box 457, Ganado, AZ 86505.
 	
Michele J. Upvall, PhD, RN, Asst. Professor of Nursing; Janie Lee Hall, RN, Nurse Executive, SMH; Stephanie Horner, RN; and Marie Jim, Supervisor of Social Services.
	Clients: members of the Ganado & Grazing District 17 community, primarily Navajo.	Help to alleviate problems of youth violence, alcohol/substance abuse, graffiti, and other concerns related to youth in the community.	A collaborative effort entitled Community Mobilization Program:
			• introduction of the community to program through a kickoff meeting at the local chapter house, and identification of potential facilitators;
			• training of facilitators to conduct community mobilization meetings throughout the district; facilitators included the authors and interested members of the community, identified at the kickoff meeting;
			• use of a targeted meeting process:
			  ☞ review ground rules (e.g., all ideas are good, stay with the agenda, listen, and respect others),
			  ☞ discuss agenda (e.g., brainstorming, history of problem, barriers, action plan);
			• identification of priority concerns and development of a master problem list through meetings at multiple locations:
			  ☞ list sent to a " core planning group" consisting of facilitators and another member of individual community groups,
			  ☞ core planning group disseminates information and provides a source of support to group leaders, assisting with implementation of the action plans.

Table 10.4 continued
New Roles, Systems, and Relationships in the Practice Setting

Setting/Authors	Populations	Goals	Interventions/Strategies
6. University of Utah Hospitals and Clinics, Customer Service Department[a], 50 North Medical Drive, Salt Lake City, UT 84132. *Jackie A. Smith, PhD, Coordinator, Quality Resources.*	**Staff:** 94%, are white; largest minority group is Hispanic. **Clients:** 700 inpatients per year use Spanish as their first language; 200 use Vietnamese.	Extend a First Impressions program to two targeted community groups.	*First Impressions* is a 30-minute video and resource packet designed to educate patients on what to expect from services at the hospital: • sample sections focus on admitting, daily hospital routines, meals, pastoral care, and the discharge process; • resource packet includes, for example, information on advance directives and visitation; • local talent from a TV station enlisted to do Spanish voice-over; • early involvement with members of Vietnamese community helped with translation, as did bilingual per diem nurse. Nurse managers were given the videos and packets, and local community clinics were instrumental in distribution of the information to these diverse patient populations.

[a] For networking purposes, contact Abe Bakhsheshy, PhD, at the Customer Service Department.

Suggested Readings and Resources

The authors suggest these readings from the nursing and business literature for the reader who desires to explore the topic of managing diversity in more detail. We also have included some centralized resources for additional information. The readings/ resources are arranged topically to assist in quick reference.

1. Cultural Competence and Related Concepts

Allen, J.P. We the People: An Atlas of America's Ethnic Diversity. New York: Macmillan, 1988. Based on the 1980 census.

Allman, K.K.M. "Race, Racism, and Health: Examining the 'Natural' Facts." In Critique, Resistance, and Action: Working Papers on the Politics of Nursing. Edited by J.L. Thompson, D.G. Allen, and L. Rodrigues-Fisher, 35-52. New York: National League for Nursing, 1992.

American Academy of Nursing, Expert Panel on Culturally Competent Nursing Care. "AAN Expert Panel Report: Culturally Competent Nursing Care." Nursing Outlook 40, no. 6 (1992): 277-283. Describes assumptions, definitions, and Leininger's and Orem's theoretical models for direct research with culturally diverse groups, culture brokering (Jezewski), somatopsychic therapy (Flaskerud), and cross-cultural health promotion (Reinert) as practice models. Discussion of cultural competence in curricula and 10 recommendations.

American Nurses Association. Code for Nurses with Interpretive Statements. Kansas City, Mo.: American Nurses Association, 1985.

———. Proceedings of Invitational Meeting: Multicultural Issues in the Nursing Workforce and Workplace. Washington, D.C.: American Nurses Association, 1993. Issues and priorities are identified. Sponsored by the ANA Council on Cultural Diversity in Nursing Practice.

———. Standards for Nursing Service Administration. Washington, D.C.: American Nurses Association, 1996.

American Nurses Association, Council on Cultural Diversity in Nursing Practice. "Cultural Diversity in Nursing Practice." Position statement, Washington, D.C., 1991.

Bauwens, E.E. The Anthropology of Health. St. Louis: C.V. Mosby, 1978.

Brislin, R. Understanding Culture's Influence on Behavior. New York: Harcourt Brace Jovanovich, 1993.

Chrisman, N. "The Health Seeking Process: An Approach to the Natural History of Illness." Culture, Medicine, and Psychiatry 1, no. 4 (1977): 351-377.

Habayeb, G. "Cultural Diversity: A Nursing Concept Not Yet Reliably Defined." Nursing Outlook 43, no. 5 (1995): 224-227.

Hall, J.M.; P.E. Stevens; and A.I. Meleis. "Marginalization: A Guiding Concept for Valuing Diversity in Nursing Knowledge Development." Advances in Nursing Science 16, no. 4 (1994): 23-41.

Harwood, A., ed. Ethnicity and Medical Care. Cambridge, Mass.: Harvard University Press, 1981.

Helman, C. Culture, Health, and Illness. Bristol, England: John Wright & Sons, 1990.

Henderson, G. and M. Primeaux, eds. Transcultural Health Care. Menlo Park, Calif.: Addison-Wesley, 1981.

Leininger, M.M. Nursing and Anthropology: Two Worlds To Blend. New York: John Wiley & Sons, 1970.

————. "Transcultural Nursing: The Study and Practice Field." Imprint 38, no. 2 (1991): 55-66. The entire focus of this special issue is on transcultural nursing. Discusses definition of transcultural nursing.

Lenburg, C.B.; J.G. Lipson; A.S. Demi; D.R. Blaney; P.N. Stern; P.R. Schultz; and L. Gage. Promoting Cultural Competence in and through Nursing Education: A Critical Review and Comprehensive Plan for Action. Washington, D.C.: American Academy of Nursing, 1995.

Louie, K.B. "Transcending Cultural Bias: The Literature Speaks." Topics in Clinical Nursing 7, no. 3 (1985): 78-84. Presents concerns about cultural bias in nursing education, service, and administration, with recommendations for change.

Lowenstein, A. and C. Glanville. "Transcultural Concepts Applied to Nursing Administration." Journal of Nursing Administration 21, no. 3 (1991): 13-14.

Meleis, A.I.; M. Eisenberg; J.E. Koerner; B. Lacey; and P. Stern. Diversity, Marginalization, and Culturally Competent Health Care: Issues in Knowledge Development. Washington, D.C.: American Academy of Nursing, 1995.

Rogler, L.H. "The Meaning of Culturally Sensitive Research in Mental Health." American Journal of Psychiatry 146, no. 3 (1989): 296-303.

Silva, M.C. "The Ethics of Cultural Diversity and Culturally Competent Nursing Education, Practice, and Research." Nursing Connections 7, no. 2 (1994): 52-56.

Spector, R. Cultural Diversity in Health and Illness. 4th ed. Norwalk, Conn.: Appleton & Lange, 1996.

Tripp-Reimer, T. and M.C. Doughterty. "Cross Cultural Research." In Annual Review of Nursing Research 3. Edited by H.H. Werley and J.J. Fitzpatrick, 77-104. New York: Springer, 1985. Describes state of the research at that time.

2. Cultural Assessment

Boyle, J.S. and M.M. Andrews. Transcultural Concepts of Nursing Care. 2nd ed. Philadelphia: J.B. Lippincott, 1995. Contains Boyle's and Andrews' assessment of cultural manifestations guide.

Brink, P.H. "Value Orientation as an Assessment Tool on Cultural Diversity." Nursing Research 33, no. 4 (1984): 198-203. Suggests using Klukhohn's value orientation instrument in cross-cultural research.

————. Transcultural Nursing: A Book of Readings. Prospect Heights, Ill.: Waveland Press, 1989.

Capitman, J.A.; W. Hernandez-Gallegos; and D.L. Yee. "Diversity Assessments in Aging Services." Generations 15, no. 4 (1991): 73-76.

Dobson, S.M. Transcultural Nursing. London: Scutari Press, 1991.

Fong, C.M. "Ethnicity and Nursing Practice." Topics in Clinical Nursing 7, no. 3 (1985): 1- 10. Contains the CONFHER cultural assessment guide.

Geissler, E., ed. Cultural Assessment: Pocket Guide. St. Louis: C.V. Mosby, 1995.

Giger, J.N. and R.E. Davidhizar, eds. Transcultural Nursing: Assessment and Intervention. 2nd ed. St. Louis: Mosby Year Book, 1995. Contains a conceptual framework for cultural assessment and intervention.

Grote, K. Diversity Awareness Profile. San Diego: Pfeiffer & Co., 1991.

Henderson, D.J. "Cultural Sensitivity in Nursing." MNRS Connection 6, no. 3 (1990): 6.

Leininger, M. Transcultural Nursing: Concepts, Theories, and Practices. New York: John Wiley & Sons, 1978. Contains a transcultural health model for analyzing health-illness systems in different cultures.

. "Leininger's Theory of Nursing: Cultural Care Diversity and Universality." Nursing Science Quarterly 1, no. 4 (1988): 152-160. Contains a transcultural health model for analyzing health-illness systems in different cultures.

. Culture Care Diversity and Universality: A Theory of Nursing. New York: National League for Nursing, 1991.

Lowenstein, A.J. and C. Glanville. "Cultural Diversity and Conflict in the Health Care Workplace." Nursing Economic$ 13, no. 4 (1995): 203-209. Contains a model for assessment and intervention in racial and status conflicts in hospital settings.

Orque, M.S.; B. Black; and L.S. Ahumada-Monrroy. Ethnic Nursing Care. St. Louis: C.V. Mosby, 1983. Contains comprehensive assessment information.

Simons, G.F. The Questions of Diversity. ODT Inc., 1994; distributed by Intercultural Press, Yarmouth, Maine. Questionnaires and diagnostic forms for assessing organizational readiness for diversity training.

Tripp-Reimer, T.; P.J. Brink; and J.M. Sanders. "Cultural Assessment: Content and Process." Nursing Outlook 32, no. 2 (1984): 78-82. Contains the Tripp-Reimer Assessment, which is a synthesis of nine cultural assessment guides. Also reprinted in: Spradley, B.S., ed. Readings in Community Health Nursing. New York: J.B. Lippincott, 1991.

3. Gender and Sexual Orientation Among Nursing Personnel

American Medical Association, Council on Ethical and Judicial Affairs. 1994. "Gender Discrimination in the Medical Profession." Women's Health Institute 4, no. 1 (1994): 1-11.

Butter, I.E. Sex and Status: Hierarchies in the Health Workforce. Washington, D.C.: American Public Health Association, 1985.

Butter, I.E.; B.K. Carpenter; and R. Simmons. "Gender Hierarchies in the Health Labor Force." International Journal of Health Services 17, no. 1 (1987): 133-149.

Fagenson, E. Women in Management. Newbury Park, Calif.: Sage, 1993.

Fee, E. Women and Health: The Politics of Sex in Medicine. Farmingdale, N.Y.: Baywood, 1983.

Hooks, b. Yearning: Race, Gender, and Cultural Politics. Boston: South End Press, 1990.

James, K.; C. Lovato; and G. Khoo. "Social Identity Correlates of Minority Workers' Health." Academy of Management Journal 37, no. 2 (1994): 383-396.

Lefkowitz, J. "Sex-Related Differences in Job Attitudes and Dispositional Variables: Now You See Them...." Academy of Management Journal 37, no. 2 (1994): 323-349.

Lorber, J. and S.A. Farrell. The Social Construction of Gender. Newbury Park, Calif.: Sage, 1990.

Morrison, A.M. The New Leaders: Guidelines on Leadership Diversity in America. San Francisco: Jossey-Bass, 1992.

Morrison A.M. and M.A. von Glinow. "Women and Minorities in Management." American Psychologist 45, no. 2 (1990): 200-208.

Muller, H.J. and C. Cocotas. "Women and Power: New Leadership in the Health Industry." Healthcare for Women International 9, no. 2 (1988): 63-82.

Porter-O'Grady, T. "Reverse Discrimination in Nursing Leadership: Hitting the Concrete Ceiling." Nursing Administration Quarterly 19, no. 2 (1995): 56-62.

Powell, G. Women and Men in Management. 2nd ed. Thousand Oaks, Calif.: Sage, 1993.

Stevens, P.E.; J.M. Hall; and A.I. Meleis. "Examining Vulnerability of Women Clerical Workers from Five Ethnic/Racial Groups." Western Journal of Nursing Research 14 (1992): 754-774.

Tannen, D. You Just Don't Understand: Women and Men in Conversation. New York: Ballentine, 1990.

Thernstrom, S., ed. Harvard Encyclopedia of American Ethnic Groups. Cambridge, Mass.: Harvard University Press, Belknap Press, 1980. Massive and comprehensive reference source covering 100 ethnic groups in the United States.

4. Immigrants as Nursing Personnel

Martin, K.; D. Wimberley; and K. O'Keefe. "Resolving Conflict in a Multicultural Nursing Department." Nursing Management 25, no. 1 (1994): 49-51. Reports on a funded project for developing and implementing a cultural assimilation core curriculum focusing on team building. Includes three modules: "Cultural Diversity," "Welcome to America," and "Cultural Diversity: Making it Work for You."

Pilette, P. "Recruitment and Retention of International Nurses Aided by Recognition of Phases of the Adjustment Process." Journal of Continuing Education in Nursing 20, no. 6 (1989): 277-281.

5. Systems to Provide Culturally Competent Care to Patients from Differing Cultures

American Psychological Association. Guidelines for Providers of Psychological Services to Ethnic and Culturally Diverse Populations. Washington, D.C.: American Psychological Association, 1991.

Anderson, J.M. "Health Care Across Cultures." Nursing Outlook 38, no. 3 (1990): 136-139. Contains a negotiation model based on one developed by Kleinman 1978. Tripp-Reimer's model also is based on Kleinman's model.

Arriaga, R. "Risk Management: Cross-Cultural Considerations." REHAB Management 7, no. 5 (August/September 1994): 99-101, 131.

Bonaparte, B.H. "Ego Defensiveness, Open/Closed Mindedness, and Nurses' Attitudes." Nursing Research 28, no. 3 (1979): 166-172.

Branch, M.F. and P.P. Paxton. Providing Safe Nursing Care for Ethnic People of Color. New York: Appleton-Century-Crofts, 1976.

Budman, D.; J. Lipson; and A.I. Meleis. "The Cultural Consultant in Mental Health Care: The Case of an Arab Adolescent." American Journal of Orthopsychiatry 10, no. 23 (1991): 1-13.

Bushey, A. "Cultural and Ethnic Diversity: Cultural Competence." In Advanced Practice Nursing. Edited by J.V. Hickey, 91-106. Philadelphia: Lippincott-Raven, 1996.

Campinha-Bacote, J. The Process of Cultural Competence: A Culturally Competent Model of Care. Wyoming, Ohio: Transcultural CARE Associates, 1991.

Capers, C.F., ed. "Cultural Diversity and Nursing Practice." Topics in Clinical Nursing special issue 7, no. 3 (1985).

Collins, J.E. PRIME. White Plains, N.Y.: March of Dimes Birth Defects Foundation, Education and Health Promotion Department, 1991. An interactive training program for reducing infant mortality through empowerment of the mothers; primarily aimed at Hispanic women.

COSSMHO. Delivering Preventive Health Care to Hispanics: A Manual for Providers. Washington, D.C.: National Coalition of Hispanic Health and Human Service Organizations, 1988.

Cross, T.L.; B.J. Bazon; K.W. Dennis; and M.R. Isaacs. Toward a Culturally Competent System of Care. Washington, D.C.: Georgetown University Child Development Center, 1989.

DeSantis, L. "Developing Faculty Expertise in Culturally Focused Care and Research." Journal of Professional Nursing 7, no. 5 (1991): 300-309.

Education Program Associates. Campbell, Calif. A state-funded resource center to search out, select, and evaluate health education materials that are culturally appropriate. Serves only the state of California.

Eliason, M. "Ethics and Transcultural Nursing Care." Nursing Outlook 41 (1993): 225-228.

Galanti, G.A. Caring for Patients from Different Cultures. Philadelphia: University of Pennsylvania Press, 1991. Contains case studies of cultural conflicts and suggestions for resolution.

Green, J.W., ed. Cultural Awareness in the Human Services. Englewood Cliffs, N.J.: Prentice Hall, 1982.

Jezewski, M.A. "Culture Brokering in Migrant Farm Workers' Health Care." Western Journal of Nursing Research 12, no. 54 (1990): 497-513.

Kleinman, A.; L. Eisenberg; and B. Good. "Culture Illness and Care: Clinical Lessons." Annals of Internal Medicine 88 (1978): 251-258.

LaFargue, J.P. "Mediating Between Two Views of Illness." Topics in Clinical Nursing 7, no. 3 (1985): 70-77. Includes a case example using culture brokering.

Maternal and Child Health Bureau. MCH Program Interchange: Focus on Ethnocultural Diversity in MCH Programs. Washington, D.C.: U.S. Department of Health and Human Services, National Center for Education in Maternal and Child Health, 1991. Describes information available from federal, state, and local agencies, as well as other organizations. The address is NCCMCH, 38th & R St., N.W., Washington, D.C. 20057. Telephone no. 202-625-8400.

Meleis, A.; J. Hall; and P. Stevens. "Scholarly Caring in Doctoral Nursing

Education: Promoting Diversity and Collaborative Mentorship." Image 26, no. 3 (1994): 177-180.

Orlandi, M., ed. Cultural Competence for Evaluators: A Guide for Alcohol and Other Drug Abuse Prevention Practitioners Working with Ethnic/Racial Communities. Rockville, Md.: U.S. Department of Health and Human Services, 1992. ADAMHA Office for Substance Abuse Prevention publication # (ADM) 92-1884. Distributed by OSAP National Clearinghouse for Alcohol and Drug Abuse Information, P.O. Box 2345, Rockville, Md. 20847-2345.

Pyles, S.H. and P.N. Stern. "Discovery of Nursing Gestalt in Critical Care Nursing: The Importance of the Grey Gorilla Syndrome." IMAGE: The Journal of Nursing Scholarship 15 (1982): 51-57.

Randall-David, E. Strategies for Working with Culturally Diverse Communities and Clients. Washington, D.C.: Association for the Care of Children's Health, 1989.

Spector, R.E. Cultural Diversity in Health and Illness. 3rd ed. Norwalk, Conn.: Appleton & Lange, 1991. Describes different perceptions of patients and providers, and suggests ways to handle potential problem areas.

Sue, D.W. Counseling the Culturally Different: Theory and Practice. New York: John Wiley & Sons, 1981.

Thiederman, S.B. "Ethnocentrism: A Barrier to Effective Health Care." Nurse Practitioner 11, no. 8 (1986): 53-59. A brief questionnaire to check cultural values. Describes the impact of ethnocentrism on primary care.

Tripp-Reimer, T. "Cross-Cultural Perspectives on Patient Teaching." Nursing Clinics of North America 24, no. 3 (1989): 613-619.

6. Culturally Competent Teamwork

Alexander, J.; R. Lichtenstein; K. Jinnett; T.A. D'Aunno; and E. Ullman. "The Effects of Treatment Team Diversity and Size on Assessments of Team Functioning." Hospital and Health Services Administration 41, no. 1 (1996): 37-53.

Asante, M.K. and W.B. Gudykunst, eds. Handbook of International and Intercultural Communication. Newbury Park, Calif.: Sage, 1989.

Burner, O.; P. Cunningham; and H. Hater. "Managing a Multicultural Nursing Staff in a Multicultural Environment." Journal of Nursing Administration 20, no. 6 (1990): 30-34.

Hall, E.T. The Silent Language. Garden City, N.Y.: Anchor Books, 1976.

Husting, P.M. "Managing a Culturally Diverse Workforce." Nursing Management 26, no. 8 (1995): 26-32. Includes a four-phase framework for measuring organizational progress in culturally congruent management.

Jackson, S.E.; V.K. Stone; and E.B. Alvarez. "Socialization Amidst Diversity: The Impact of Demographics on Workteam Oldtimers and Newcomers." Research in Organizational Behavior 15 (1992): 45-109.

Jein, R. and B. Harris. "Cross-Cultural Conflict: The American Nurse Manager and Culturally Mixed Staff." Journal of New York State Nurses Association 20, no. 2 (1989): 16-18.

Leininger, M.M. "Becoming Aware of Types of Health Care Practitioners and Cultural Imposition." Journal of Transcultural Nursing 2, no. 2 (1991): 32-39.

Moran, T.R. "Getting Everyone to Pull Together in Multicultural Firms." International Management 40, no. 5 (1985): 74.

O'Reilly, C.A.; D. Caldwell; and W. Barnett. "Workgroup Demography, Social Integration, and Turnover." Administrative Science Quarterly 34, no. 1 (1989): 21-37.

Poole, V.L.; J.N. Giger; and R.E. Davidhizar. "Delegating to a Transcultural Team." Nursing Management 26, no. 8 (1995): 33-34.

Tellis-Nayak, V. and M. Tellis-Nayak. "Quality of Care and the Burden of Two Cultures: When the World of the Nurse's Aide Enters the World of the Nursing Home." The Gerontologist 29, no. 3 (1989): 307-313.

7. Managing Intercultural Business Encounters

Barbee, E.L. "Tensions in the Brokerage Role: Nurses in Botswana." Western Journal of Nursing Research 9, no. 2 (1987): 244-256.

Barham, K. and M. Devine. The Quest for the International Manager: A Survey of Global Human Resource Strategies. London: Business Press, 1991.

Bartlett, C. and G. Sumatra. Managing Across Cultures. Boston: Harvard Business School Press, 1987.

Brown, B.J. "A World View of Nursing Practice: An International Perspective." In The Nursing Profession: Turning Points. Edited by N. Chaska, 406-414. St. Louis: C.V. Mosby, 1990.

, ed. "Corporate Nursing and Consultants." Nursing Administration Quarterly special issue 10, no. 4 (summer 1986).

. "International Nursing Administration." Nursing Administration Quarterly special issue 16, no. 2 (winter 1992).

Elashmawi, F. and P.R. Harris. Multicultural Management: New Skills for Global Success. Houston: Gulf Publishing, 1993.

Henry, B., ed. International Administration of Nursing Services. Philadelphia: The Charles Press, 1989.

Kras, E. Management in Two Cultures. Yarmouth, Maine: Intercultural Press, 1989. Pinpoints principal differences between the culture and management styles of Americans and Mexicans.

Parker Pen Company. Do's and Taboos Around the World: A Guide to International Behavior. New York: Benjamin Co., 1985.

Rhinesmith, S. A Manager's Guide to Globalization. Homewood, Ill.: Business One Irwin, 1992.

8. Models of Organizational Structures and Processes to Improve Organizational Multicultural Competence

Clark, L. and D. Waltzman, eds. Faculty and Student Challenges in Facing Cultural and Linguistic Diversity. Springfield, Ill.: Charles Thomas, 1986.

Colson, P., ed. Creating a Multi-Ethnic Workforce: The Challenge to Voluntary Mental Health Agencies. New York: Coalition of Voluntary Mental Retardation and Alcoholism Agencies, Ethnic Affairs Committee, 1990.

Cox, T. "The Multicultural Organization." Academy of Management Executives 5, no. 2 (1991): 34-47.

_. Cultural Diversity in Organizations. San Francisco: Barrett-Koehler, 1993.

Cushner, K. and G. Trifonovitch. "Understanding, Misunderstanding: Barriers to Dealing with Diversity." Social Education 53, no. 5 (1989): 318-322.

Eubanks, P. "Workforce Diversity in Health Care: Managing the Melting Pot." Hospitals 64, no. 12 (1990): 48-50, 66.

Fernandez, J.P. Managing a Diverse Workforce: Regaining the Competitive Edge. Lexington, Mass.: Lexington, 1991.

Frieden, J. 1990. "Valuing Diversity: Ways to Answer Minority Needs." Business and Health (January 1990): 32-34.

Gentile, M.C. Differences that Work: Organizational Excellence through Diversity. Cambridge, Mass.: Harvard Business School Press, 1994. Reprints of 14 articles and three cases from Harvard Business Review between 1973 and 1991, with the conclusion that companies that see diversity as a process to be managed unleash performance energy that was previously wasted on fighting discrimination. Diversity is described as encompassing gender, race, age, disability, AIDS, families, etc.

Harris, P. and R. Moran. Managing Cultural Differences. Houston: Gulf Publishing, 1990.

Hofstede, G. Cultures and Organizations. London: McGraw-Hill, 1991.

Howard, R. "Values Make the Company: An Interview with Robert Haas." Harvard Business Review 68, no. 5 (1990): 133-144.

Jackson, B.W. and E. Holvino. "Developing Multicultural Organizations." Journal of Religion and the Applied Behavioral Sciences 9, no. 4 (1988): 14-19.

Jackson, S. Diversity in the Workplace. New York: Guilford, 1992.

. "Team Composition in Organizational Settings: Issues in Managing an Increasingly Diverse Workforce." In Group Process and Productivity. Edited by S. Worchel, W. Wood, and J.A. Simpson, 138-173. Newbury Park, Calif.: Sage, 1992.

Jamieson, D. and J. O'Mara. Managing Workforce 2000: Gaining the Diversity Advantage. San Francisco: Jossey-Bass, 1991.

Kavanagh, K.H. and P.H. Kennedy. Promoting Cultural Diversity: Strategies for Health Care Professionals. Newbury Park, Calif.: Sage, 1992. Includes 12 case studies, workshop interventions, and an overview of the concept.

Kennedy, J. and A. Everist. "Put Diversity into Context." Personnel Journal 70, no. 9 (1991): 50-54.

Kerfoot, K.M. "Managing Cultural Diversity: Turning Demographic Factors into a Competitive Advantage." Nursing Economic$ 8, no. 5 (1990): 354-362.

Kossek, E.E. and S.C. Zonia. "Assessing Diversity Climates: A Field Study of Reactions to Employer Efforts to Promote Diversity." Journal of Organizational Behavior 14, no. 14 (1993): 61-81.

Loden, M. and R.H. Loeser. "Working Diversity: Managing the Differences." Bureaucrat 20, no. 1 (1991): 21-25.

Loden, M. and J.B. Rosener. Workforce America! Managing Employee Diversity as a Vital Resource. Homewood, Ill.: Business One Irwin, 1991.

Malone, B.L. "Caring for Culturally Diverse Racial Groups: An Administrative Matter." Nursing Administration Quarterly 17, no. 2 (1993): 21-29.

Mills, A.J. and P. Tancred. Gendering Organizational Analysis. Newbury Park, Calif.: Sage, 1992.

Morrison, A.M. The New Leaders: Guidelines on Leadership Diversity as a Vital Resource. Homewood, Ill.: Business One Irwin, 1991.

Morrison, A.M. and K.M. Crabtree, eds. Developing Diversity in Organizations: A Digest of Selected Literature. Greensboro, N.C.: Center for Creative Leadership, 1992.

Muller, H.J. and B.E. Haase. "Managing Diversity in Health Services Organizations." Hospital and Health Services Administration 39, no. 4 (1994): 415-434.

Nkomo, S.M. "The Emperor Has No Clothes: Rewriting Race in Organizations." Academy of Management Review 17, no. 3 (1992): 487-513.

Simons, G.F.; C. Vazquez; and P.R. Harris. Transcultural Leadership: Empowering the Diverse Workforce. Houston: Gulf Publishing, 1993.

Sukela, T.A. and G.C. Crosier. Managing the Mosaic: Addressing Workforce Diversity and Managing Institutional Change in Health Care. Chicago: American Hospital Publishing, 1994. Describes the increasingly varied work force and the application of concepts from anthropology and sociology to management. Six appendices are presented to assist the reader in applying the concepts.

Thiederman, S. "Managing and Motivating the Culturally Diverse Work Force." In 1993 Annual: Developing Human Resources. 201-211. San Diego:
Pfeiffer, 1993. Based on material from author's books: (1) Bridging Cultural Barriers for Corporate Success, New York: Lexington/Macmillan, 1991, and (2) Profiting in America's Multicultural Marketplace, New York: Lexington/Macmillan, 1991.

Thomas Jr., R.R. "From Affirmative Action to Affirming Diversity." Harvard Business Review 68, no. 2 (1990): 107-117.

———. Beyond Race and Gender. New York: American Management Association, 1991.

———. "Managing Diversity: A Conceptual Framework." In Diversity In the Workplace. Edited by S.E. Jackson. New York: Guilford, 1992.

Wagner, M. "Managing Diversity." Modern Healthcare 21, no. 30 (1991): 24-29.

West, E.A. "The Cultural Bridge Model." Nursing Outlook 41 (1993): 229-234.

9. Training in Cultural Sensitivity

Bafa Bafa. Available from Intercultural Press, P.O. Box 768, Yarmouth, Maine 04096.

Blackburn, J.A. "Achieving a Multicultural Service Orientation: Adaptive Models in Service Delivery and Race and Culture Training." Caring (April 1992): 22-26.

Bright Productions. Diversity: Crossing the Lines. California: Concept Media, 1994. A series of three videos: (1) Make Contact (describes the immigrant experience and roots of prejudice in U.S. society), (2) Make a Move (explores personal stories of those experiencing prejudice and the media's role), and (3) Make a Difference (describes successful programs in organizations to increase ethnic and cultural understanding). Telephone no. 800-233-7078.

Brookdale Center on Aging, Hunter College, 425 East 25th Street, New York, N.Y. 10010. Publications include home health aide training manuals (with a chapter on intercultural dynamics), video reviews (HRI-201 = "Cultural Perspectives on Aging").

Brown, C.R. and G.J. Mazza. "Peer Training Strategies for Welcoming Diversity." National Coalition Building Institute International, Washington, D.C., 1992.

Casse, P. Training for the Multicultural Manager. Yarmouth, Maine: Intercultural Press, 1982.

Eliason, M.J. and N.M. Macy. "A Classroom Activity to Introduce Cultural Diversity." Nurse Educator 17 (1992): 32-36.

Fischer, P.Z. "Teaching About Cultural Diversity to Health Administration Students: A Teaching Module." The Journal of Health Administration Education 13, no. 2 (1995): 305-319.

Gorrie, M. "Reaching Clients through Cross-Cultural Education." Journal of Gerontological Nursing 15, no. 10 (1989): 29-31. Describes a staff development program to orient new staff to culturally specific nursing care.

Hall, B.P.; B. Taylor; J. Kalven; and L.S. Rosen. Developing Human Values. International Values Institute of Marian College, 1982.

Hummel, F. and D. Peters. "Bafa, Bafa: A Cultural Awareness Game." Nurse Educator 19, no. 2 (1994): 8.

Huttlinger, K. and S.B. Keating. "Understanding Cultural Diversity through a Student Exchange Program." Nurse Educator 16, no. 5 (1991): 29-33.

Johnson, R.B. and J. O'Mara. "Shedding New Light on Diversity Training." Training and Development (May 1992): 45-52. Describes key behaviors and phases of training.

Kanter, R.M. Tale of "O": On Being Different in an Organization. Produced by Barry Stein. Cambridge, Mass.: Goodmeasure Direct, Inc., One Memorial Drive, Cambridge, Mass. 02142. Video-cassette in 18- and 30-minute versions.

Karp, J.B. "The Emotional Impact and a Model for Changing Racist Attitudes." In Impacts of Racism on White Americans. Edited by B.P. Bowser and R.B. Hunt. Beverly Hills, Calif.: Sage, 1981.

Karp, J.B. and N. Sutton. "Where Diversity Training Goes Wrong." Training (July 1993): 30- 34.

Katz, J.H. White Awareness Handbook for Anti-Racist Training. Norman, Okla.: University of Oklahoma Press, 1978.

Kogod, S.K. A Workshop for Managing Diversity in the Workplace. San Diego: Pfeiffer & Co., 1991. Assessment of cultural bias and 18 activities with specific instructions on how to do workshops of varying length. No suggested readings. A chapter based on the workshop is published in 1992 Annual: Developing Human Resources, Pfeiffer & Co., 8517 Production Avenue, San Diego, Calif. 92121. Telephone no. 619-578-5900.

Kohls, R.L. and J.M. Knight. Developing Intercultural Awareness. 2nd ed. Yarmouth, Maine: Intercultural Press, 1994. Outlines designs of one- and two-day cultural awareness workshops, with 21 resource sections.

Ledfley, H. and P. Peterson, eds. Cross-Cultural Training for Mental Health Professionals. Springfield, Ill.: Charles C. Thomas, 1986.

Multus, Inc. Conference Diversophy. Yarmouth, Maine: Intercultural Press, 1993. A simulation game; short and long versions available for training.

National Institute on Human Resources and Aging, 425 East 25th Street, New York, N.Y. 10010. Telephone no. 212-481-4350. Identifies "best practices" in staff recruitment, training, management/supervision, and publishing in quarterly newsletter, Human Resources and Aging. Information packets and filmographies available; keeps vertical files by topic, including "Managing Cultural Diversity."

Powell, G.N. Gender and Diversity in the Workplace: Learning Activities and Exercises. Thousand Oaks, Calif.: Sage, 1994. Collection of training activities for increasing cultural sensitivity and awareness of the work process and legal implications.

Raff, B.S. and E. Fiore. Culturally Sensitive Caregiving and Childbearing Families. Module 1. White Plains, N.Y.: March of Dimes Birth Defects Foundation, 1992. A training program for staff development, available through Education and Health Promotion Department, March of Dimes, 1275 Mamaroneck Avenue, White Plains, N.Y. 10605.

Shirts, G.R. BaFa, BaFa: A Cross-Cultural Simulation Game. Del Mar, Calif.: Simile, 1976.

Simons, G.F. Working Together. Crisp Publications, 1989; distributed by Intercultural Press, Yarmouth, Maine. Case studies and work sheets for use in workshops.

Stanford Geriatric Education Center, 703 Welch Road, Suite H-1, Stanford, Calif. 94305. Offerings include Geriatric Assessment: A Functionally Oriented, Ethnically Sensitive Approach to the Older Patient (20-minute video produced by E. Segal), and "Ethnicity and Nursing Homes: Components of Culturally Sensitive Care" (SGEC Working Paper #9, by G. Yeo).

Storti, C. The Art of Crossing Cultures. Yarmouth, Maine: Intercultural Press, 1994.

Tatem, B.D. "Talking about Race, Learning about Racism: The Application of Racial Identity Development Theory in the Classroom." Harvard Educational Review 62, no. 2 (1992): 1-24.

Thiagarajan, S. and B. Stienwachs. Barnga: A Simulation Game on Cultural Clashes. Yarmouth, Maine: Intercultural Press, 1990. A card game.

Wallace, P.E.; C.M. Ermer; and D.N. Motshabi. "Managing Diversity: A Senior Management Perspective." Hospital and Health Services Administration 41, no. 1 (1996): 91-104. Published survey of urban hospital CEOs shows consensus that diversity exists in the work force, yet only 30% have instituted programs to manage diversity.

Williams, J. and S. Rogers. "The Multicultural Workplace: Preparing Preceptors." The Journal of Continuing Education in Nursing 24, no. 3 (1993): 101-104.